BE STRONG

Strength Training for Muscular Fitness
For Men and Women

WAYNE WESTCOTT, Ph.D.
South Shore YMCA

WCB Brown &
Benchmark

Wayne Westcott, Ph.D., strength training consultant for:

YMCA of the USA
IDEA: The Association for Fitness Professionals
American Council on Exercise
National Youth Sports Foundation
National Academy of Sports Medicine

Formerly strength training consultant for the President's Council on Physical Fitness and Sport and faculty member at Eastern Connecticut State University, Pennsylvania State University, and Florida State University.

Library of Congress Cataloging in Publication Data:
    WESTCOTT, WAYNE 1949 –
    BE STRONG: STRENGTH TRAINING FOR MUSCULAR FITNESS FOR MEN AND WOMEN

Cover Design: Phill Thill

Copy Editor: Kathy Childers

Production Manager: Joanne Cooper

Library of Congress Catalog Card number: 92-82760
ISBN: 0-697-13073-8

Printed in the United States of America by Brown & Benchmark, 2460 Kerper Boulevard, Dubuque, IA 52001.

10 9 8 7 6 5 4 3

Contents

Dedication

To my wife, Claudia, and our parents, for their prayers and encouragement, with special appreciation for my mother, Eva Westcott.

Acknowledgments

I greatly appreciate the ability and assistance of the individuals most responsible for this book. They are: my editorial directors — Ed Bartell, Karla Blaser, Stephen Lehman, Kathy Childers, and Joanne Cooper; my exercise models — Doug Pratt, Dawn Pratt, and Claudia Westcott; my typist, Susan Ramsden; my artist, Leslie Willis; my photographer, Kevin Forte; and Patricia Ryan, for her helpful reviews of my manuscripts. Thank you all for your dedication to excellence and your hard work on behalf of *Be Strong*.

Introduction

When asked about strength training, most people believe it's only important for bodybuilders, weightlifters, or football players. Unfortunately, they don't understand that strength training, or muscular fitness, is important for everyone.

Oddly enough, many adults fear having too much muscle, an unlikely occurrence. In fact, they should fear having too little muscle. Men and women who do not perform regular strength exercise lose about five pounds of muscle every 10 years. This steady loss of active tissue results in a 5 percent reduction in their metabolic rate every decade.

This is the main reason Americans can eat the same amount of food but add fat weight year after year. With less muscle tissue, calories that were previously used for muscle maintenance are now deposited into fat storage.

Can strength training change this situation? Absolutely! My research participants routinely add three pounds of muscle after two months of strength exercise. At the same time they lose three to six pounds of fat, without changing their eating patterns.

But there are many other reasons everyone should perform sensible strength training. Strong low-back muscles are the best defense against low-back discomfort, a problem four out of every five Americans encounter.

In addition, muscles function as the body's engine, chassis, and shock absorber. That is, well-conditioned muscles increase physical capacity, enhance personal appearance, and reduce injury risk.

While a reasonable amount of effort and commitment are necessary to attain muscular fitness, strength training need not be a time-consuming activity. Generally speaking, 20-30 minutes three times per week of properly performed strength exercise is sufficient to develop all major muscle groups.

Of course, a safe and productive strength training program is dependent upon sound exercise principles and correct exercise technique. *Be Strong* is designed to provide this essential information as clearly and completely as possible. As you read and apply the concepts presented herein, you should experience excellent training results and achieve a high level of muscular fitness.

1
Strength Training Overview

What is strength training? Many people think it is what you do to develop big muscles. While this may be true for a small number of competitive bodybuilders, few people have the potential to develop large muscles even if they train in a weight room three hours every day. Regardless of what you may read in magazine ads, no amount of strength training will make the average man or woman into a Mr. or Miss Olympia.

Then what is the purpose of strength training? Strong muscles make you look better, feel better, and function better. Consider this: The characteristics of a healthy body are much like what you look for in a new car — good looks, solid ride, and plenty of power. To get this in a car, you rely on the construction and reputation of the maker. To get this in your body, you rely on strength training.

But don't you need to spend a lot of time strength training to obtain these benefits? Definitely not. Numerous research studies have demonstrated that strength development requires very little time, as long as you train properly.

PROGRESSIVE RESISTANCE EXERCISE

The key to gaining strength is progressive resistance exercise. This means to gradually add resistance to training exercises.

One of the best examples of progressive resistance training is Milo of Crotona, who carried a full-grown bull on his shoulders across the Olympic stadium in ancient Greece. How did Milo develop the strength to perform this remarkable feat? He simply carried the bull a short distance on his shoulders every day, from its birth. Because the bull gained a little weight daily, Milo lifted a slightly heavier resistance during each exercise session. Milo's muscles responded to the gradual increases in resistance by becoming stronger.

Although the story of Milo may contain some exaggeration, it clearly illustrates the principle of progressive resistance. You will note that Milo's strength training program increased in effort but did not increase in time.

Quite simply, when a muscle is stressed beyond its normal demands it responds either positively or negatively. If the training stimulus is a little higher than normal, the muscle responds positively and becomes a little stronger. If the training stimulus is a lot higher than normal, the muscle responds negatively and experiences some degree of injury. It is therefore essential to train in a systematic manner, with gradual increases in the exercise resistance.

STRENGTH TRAINING FEATURES

The most important features of sensible and successful strength training are safety, effectiveness, and efficiency.

Safety: Regardless of how well a strength training program may appear to work, if it has a high risk of injury it should be avoided. For example, fast weight-lifting movements are not recommended because they place excessive stress on your muscles, tendons, and joints. Instead, you should always perform strength exercises in a slow and controlled manner.

Effectiveness: Although different conditioning programs produce some degree of strength development, some are more effective than others. Consider traditional calisthenics such as push-ups and sit-ups. Because these body weight exercises do not permit progressive resistance, they produce only modest strength gains. You can attain much better results by isolating individual muscle groups and gradually increasing the exercise resistance with dumbbells, barbells, or weight-stack machines.

Efficiency: If you are a busy person with limited time for physical conditioning, exercise efficiency is a very practical training consideration. For example, research shows that one set of strength exercise produces the same results as three sets. This being the case, single-set strength training may be the preferred exercise program for you.

The remaining chapters provide important information for understanding and applying essential strength training concepts. You will find research-based recommendations for exercise selection, sets, repetitions, intensity, progression, speed, range, frequency, breathing, and performance.

Upon completion of this book, you should be able to design a personal and productive strength training program that will enhance all of your major muscle areas (see Figures 1-1 and 1-2).

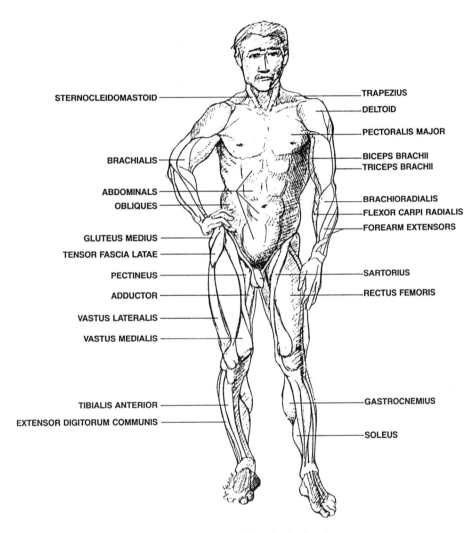

Figure 1-1. Muscles of the body: front.

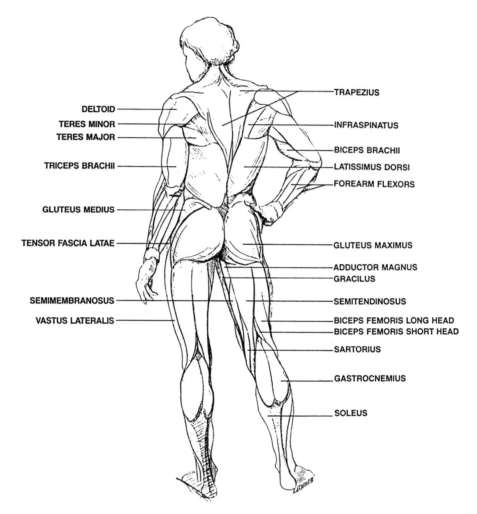

Figure 1-2. Muscles of the body: back.

2
Strength Training Benefits

There are some activities you just feel good about performing because you know they are beneficial. Strength training is one of them. After completing a strength training session, you experience a sense of physical accomplishment and personal well-being. That's because your muscles are your engines, and a sound strength workout is similar to a good tune-up.

From a physical perspective alone, strength training produces a number of important benefits. First, muscle fibers become larger and stronger, which increases their ability to produce force. Second, tendons, ligaments, and bones become denser and stronger, which increases their ability to withstand stress. These positive adaptations result in a strong and injury-resistant muscular system.

Although strength training is essential for developing larger and stronger muscles, very few individuals have the potential to become competitive body-builders or weightlifters. Nonetheless, sensible strength training can benefit just about everyone with regard to improved physical capacity, higher metabolic function, more athletic power, lower injury risk, and enhanced physical appearance.

PHYSICAL CAPACITY

Physical capacity may be defined as your ability to perform work or exercise. While your heart functions as your fuel pump, your muscles serve as your engines.

5

It is in your muscles where combustion takes place, energy is released, movement originates, and power is produced. Regular strength training increases your ability to perform work or exercise by building bigger and better muscular engines.

It is important to understand that every physical activity requires a certain percentage of your maximum physical capacity. Because your muscle strength and muscle endurance are closely related, more muscle strength automatically results in more muscle endurance. That is, strength training enables you to perform previously difficult tasks with considerably less effort.

Even sedentary individuals use a significant amount of muscle strength during the course of a day. For example, one research study found that persons who simply sit at desks from 9:00 A.M. to 5:00 P.M. lose about 40 percent of their neck strength during that time (see Figure 2-1). This is due to the fact that neck muscles hold the head erect throughout the day, and that can cause considerable muscle fatigue.

Fortunately, it does not take long to experience the effects of progressive strength training on physical capacity. It is not uncommon to observe a 20-40 percent improvement in muscle performance during the first month of strength exercise. Strong muscles enhance your physical capacity, and your physical capacity has a major influence on your daily lifestyle.

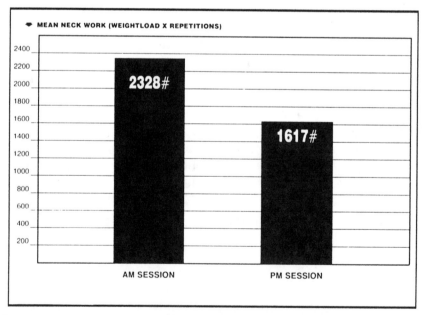

Figure 2-1. Neck strength for persons who sit at desks all day as tested at 9:00 A.M. and 5:00 P.M. (10 subjects).

METABOLIC FUNCTION

Because your muscles are your engines, strength training can have a significant influence on your metabolic function. Like other forms of exercise, strength training is a vigorous, calorie-burning activity. During a serious strength training session, your heart rate, blood pressure, and energy metabolism increase considerably. Of course, this temporary elevation in energy consumption is experienced during other large muscle activities such as running, cycling, and swimming. However, shortly after you stop these activities, your metabolism returns to its resting level.

Strength training is different because it influences your resting metabolism as well as your exercise metabolism. This is due to the fact that strength training adds muscle tissue, and muscle tissue has a high energy requirement. The more muscle you develop, the more energy you need 24 hours a day for tissue maintenance and building. Even when you are asleep, your muscles are responsible for over 25 percent of your total calorie utilization.

After age 20, men and women who do not strength train lose approximately one-half pound of muscle every year of life through lack of use. This gradual reduction in muscle tissue is largely responsible for a ½ percent per year decrease in metabolism. Strength training is the best means for maintaining your muscle mass and metabolic function throughout middle age.

Strength exercise is unique due to its double effect on energy utilization. First, strength training produces a large increase in metabolic rate during the workout. Second, strength training adds more muscle tissue, which produces a small increase in metabolic rate throughout the day.

For these reasons, strength training is helpful in reducing body fat. In one study, 72 men and women followed the same diet guidelines and spent the same amount of time in an exercise program (30 minutes a day, three days a week). Twenty-two subjects spent all 30 minutes performing endurance exercise. The other 50 participants divided each workout into 15 minutes of endurance exercise and 15 minutes of strength exercise. After eight weeks, the subjects who did only endurance training lost four pounds of fat. The subjects who performed both endurance and strength exercise lost 10 pounds of fat and gained two pounds of muscle, for a 12-pound improvement in their body composition (see Table 2-1). The better results obtained by the subjects who performed strength training were due in part to their increased muscle mass and metabolic rate.

I recently conducted a follow-up study to see if an exercise program alone would reduce body weight and enhance body composition. The 61 men and women in this study did not follow a diet. They exercised 40 minutes a day, three days a week, for a period of eight weeks. Each training session included 20 minutes of strength exercise and 20 minutes of endurance exercise. The participants lost six pounds of fat and gained three pounds of muscle for a nine-pound improvement in body composition (see Table 2-2).

Table 2-1. Changes in body weight, fat, muscle, and body composition for participants who performed strength and endurance exercise with dieting and participants who performed endurance exercise with dieting (72 subjects).

Subjects	Body weight change	Fat weight change	Muscle weight change	Body composition improvement
Strength and endurance exercise (n = 50)	–8.0 lbs.	–10.0 lbs.	+2.0 lbs.	12.0 lbs.
Endurance exercise (n = 22)	–4.0 lbs.	–4.0 lbs.	0 lbs.	4.0 lbs.

Even without dieting, the combination of strength and endurance exercise produced excellent results. Just remember that it is the strength exercise that adds muscle and increases metabolic rate.

ATHLETIC POWER

Successful sports performance is largely dependent upon the athlete's ability to produce power. Almost every athletic event has a power component. Power is most evident in activities such as putting a shot, punting a football, hitting a baseball, and sprinting 100 yards. But power is also involved in swimming one mile, running five miles, and cycling 25 miles.

In simplest terms, power is the combination of two factors: movement speed and movement force. Generally speaking, you can improve your performance power by increasing your movement speed, increasing your movement force, or both. Your movement speed is specific to each athletic activity and is best improved through high-quality skill training. Your movement force is dependent upon your muscle strength and is best improved through high-quality strength training. Although both power components are important for peak sports performance, it is better to practice each component separately — skill training to develop greater movement speed and strength training to develop greater movement force.

Table 2-2. Changes in body weight, fat, muscle, and body composition for participants who performed strength and endurance exercise without dieting (61 subjects).

Subjects	Body weight change	Fat weight change	Muscle weight change	Body composition improvement
Strength and endurance exercise Endurance exercise (n = 61)	–3.0 lbs.	–6.0 lbs.	+3.0 lbs.	9.0 lbs.

Consider how strength training may benefit a technical athletic skill such as driving a golf ball. The golfer may gain distance by swinging the club faster but may lose control in the process. The golfer may also gain distance by swinging the club with greater force. In this manner, the golfer may increase driving distance while maintaining striking accuracy because the basic swinging movement is not altered.

It should be noted that increased muscle strength does not hinder your movement speed or flexibility. In fact, properly performed strength training may enhance your flexibility by alternately stressing and stretching opposing muscle groups through a full range of movement.

Several years ago, athletes were typically advised to avoid strength exercise. Today, most professional, college, and high school athletic teams utilize strength specialists to design balanced strength training programs that develop strong athletes and reduce the risk of sports injuries. Sensible strength training certainly contributes to the improved athletic performances of today.

INJURY PREVENTION

The body, like an automobile, needs shock absorbers to prevent potential injuries from external forces. It also requires balancing agents to prevent potential injuries from internal forces. A well-conditioned and well-balanced muscular system serves both of these functions.

One of the best reasons for participating in a strength training program is to reduce the risk of common injuries. Since World War II, progressive resistance exercise has been the preferred method of injury rehabilitation. It is now understood that proper strength training may be equally useful for injury prevention.

A strong muscular system offers some protection against impact injuries, such as those caused by collision sports or running/jumping activities. For example, high-impact aerobics subjects the ankles, knees, hips, and back to repetitive landing forces leading to a high rate of joint injuries. Well-conditioned muscles absorb more of the impact forces, thereby reducing stress on the joint structures. The heavy emphasis on strength training by football coaches has helped reduce the number of fatal injuries in this sport.

A balanced musculoskeletal system is equally important for preventing overuse injuries. These injuries often result from doing too much work with some muscle groups and too little work with the opposing muscle groups. For example, distance runners frequently encounter overuse injuries to their knee joints. Part of the problem is that distance running overstresses the rear leg muscles and understresses the front leg muscles. This creates a front-to-back muscle imbalance that decreases knee joint stability and increases the risk of injury.

Although solutions are seldom simple, a first step is balanced strength exercise for all of the major muscle groups. When all of the muscles are strong, there is considerably less chance of one muscle group overpowering another and causing overuse injuries.

Of course, running is not unique. Every athletic event stresses some muscle groups more than others, which sets the stage for overuse injuries. Athletes should therefore perform regular strength training to maintain muscle balance, prevent overuse injuries, and improve sports performance.

Athletes are not the only people who encounter musculoskeletal injuries. Four out of every five Americans experience low-back difficulties, most of which result from muscle weakness or muscle imbalance. Because 80 percent of low-back problems are muscular in nature, sensible strength training may help prevent this common and serious problem.

Properly performed strength exercise can increase muscle strength, improve muscle balance, and reduce injury potential. However, you should understand that improperly performed strength exercise can be the cause of injury. Chapter 5 presents important guidelines for designing safe and effective strength training programs.

PHYSICAL APPEARANCE

Continuing the automobile analogy, your muscles are also similar to the chassis of a car. That is, they are largely responsible for your overall physical appearance. In fact, the main reason many people begin a strength training program is to look better. Looking fit is mostly a matter of muscle conditioning. Strength exercise stimulates your muscle fibers to increase in size and strength, thereby enhancing your muscle tone and firmness.

Consider the thousands of men and women who have participated in strength training programs during the past decade. Most have experienced favorable improvements in muscle size, muscle strength, muscle tone, and physical appearance, but few have developed unusually large muscles. This may explain why strength training is one of the most popular physical activities among adults.

Take a typical young woman who weighs 130 pounds and is 26 percent body fat. If she loses four pounds of fat and gains four pounds of muscle, she will still weigh 130 pounds but will have only 23 percent body fat. Although she could lose four pounds of fat through diet and endurance exercise, the only way she could gain four pounds of muscle is through strength exercise. And it is the four pounds of additional muscle that increases her muscle strength, improves her muscle tone, and enhances her physical appearance.

Strength training is unique in that the positive physical changes are readily apparent to you and to others. Improvements in body composition are usually noticeable after four to eight weeks of training, and these visible benefits provide excellent motivation to continue your strength training program.

Strength Potential

Contrary to advertisements in popular muscle magazines, few people who practice strength training develop championship physiques. Simply stated, the capacity to attain really large muscles depends on favorable genetic factors that few of us possess. However, everyone has the potential to look better, feel better, and function better as a result of intelligent strength training.

As presented in this chapter, strength exercise is an excellent means for developing your physical capacity, increasing your metabolic function, improving your athletic power, reducing your injury risk, and enhancing your physical appearance. Remember that your muscles serve as the engine, shock absorbers, and chassis of your body. For most people, the potential for muscular improvement is high, and the benefits of strength fitness are too important to be taken lightly.

3
Muscle Structure and Function

While you can certainly gain strength without understanding exactly how a muscle contracts, the more you know about muscle structure and function the better. How your muscles respond to strength exercise is important information that will help you attain better training results.

In simplest terms, sensible strength training provides a stimulus for muscle growth. Specifically, muscles respond to progressive resistance exercise by developing more protein filaments. The increased number of protein filaments results in larger and stronger muscles that have greater energy requirements.

MUSCLE STRUCTURE

The protein filaments that give muscle the ability to produce force consist of two basic components. As shown in Figure 3-1, there are thick protein strands, called myosin filaments, and thin protein strands, called actin filaments. Small cross-bridges connect the thick myosin filaments with the thin actin filaments. During contraction, the thin actin filaments are pulled towards the thick myosin filaments, causing the muscle to shorten (see Figure 3-2).

The myosin and actin filaments form myofibrils, which are the principle threads running throughout the muscles. As illustrated in Figure 3-3, groups of myofibrils are bound together into individual muscle fibers. In turn, muscle fi-

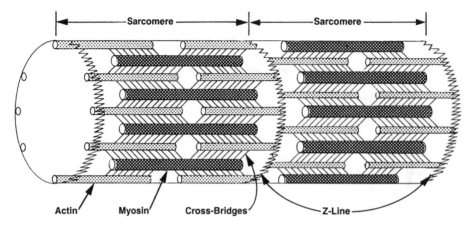

Figure 3-1. The smallest functional unit of muscle contraction, the sarcomere, consists of thin actin filaments, thick myosin filaments, and tiny cross-bridges that serve as coupling agents between the myosin proteins and the surrounding actin proteins.

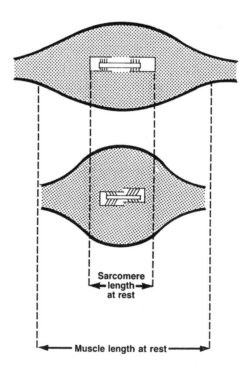

Figure 3-2. Changes in the length of individual sarcomeres and the entire muscle during concentic muscle contraction.

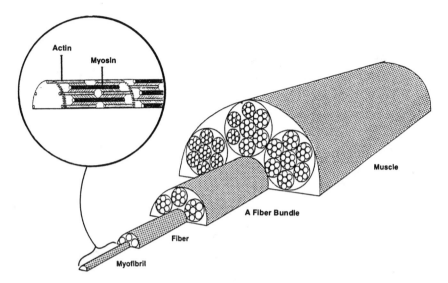

Figure 3-3. The structural and functional components of skeletal muscle.

bers are bound together into larger units known as fiber bundles. These bundles of fibers are enclosed by a connective sheath and function together as a muscle, such as the biceps.

MUSCLE FUNCTION

When a muscle is activated, it produces tension and attempts to shorten. That is, it tries to pull its attachments closer together. However, a contracting muscle may actually shorten, lengthen, or remain the same size, depending upon the force output.

Positive Contraction: When a barbell is lifted from the hip to the shoulder during the upward phase of the standing curl exercise, the biceps muscles exert force, shorten, and overcome the resistance (see Figure 3-4). Whenever muscles do this, they are said to contract positively. Positive muscle contractions are essential for overcoming the force of gravity and performing lifting movements.

Negative Contraction: When a barbell is lowered from the shoulder to the hip during the downward phase of the standing curl exercise, the biceps muscles exert force, lengthen, and are overcome by the resistance (see Figure 3-5). Whenever muscles do this, they are said to contract negatively. Negative muscle contractions are essential for reducing the force of gravity and performing controlled lowering movements. Note that if the biceps muscles did not exert force during the downward phase of the standing curl exercise, the barbell would drop in a quick, uncontrolled, and dangerous manner.

Static Contraction: When a barbell is held at the midpoint of the standing curl exercise, the biceps muscles exert force but do not change in length. They neither overcome the resistance nor are they overcome by the resistance (see Figure 3-6). Whenever a muscle exerts force but does not change in length, it is said to contract statically. Static muscle contractions are essential for matching the force of gravity and maintaining given joint positions.

Muscle Force Output

Muscle force output is most accurately measured during a static contraction, because no movement is involved. Whenever a muscle shortens, internal friction decreases the effective force output. Conversely, whenever a muscle lengthens, internal friction increases the effective force output.

For example, Mark can hold (static contraction) a 100-pound barbell at a right angle, as illustrated in Figure 3-6. Mark can slowly lift (positive contraction) an 80-pound barbell, as illustrated in Figure 3-4. Mark can slowly lower (negative contraction) a 120-pound barbell, as illustrated in Figure 3-5. In each case, Mark's muscle force production is 100 pounds. However, internal muscle friction decreases his positive force output by about 20 percent and increases his negative force output by about 20 percent. These differences in muscle force output have important implications for sensible strength training. For example, you may not be able to lift your body to the chin-up bar (positive contraction), but you can probably lower your body from the chin-up bar (negative contraction).

Prime Mover Muscles

In any given joint action, the muscle that is principally responsible for controlling the movement is termed the prime mover muscle. The prime mover muscle contracts positively when lifting a weight and negatively when lowering a weight. As an example, the biceps are the prime mover muscles for standing curls, both lifting and lowering.

Many exercises involve more than one prime mover muscle group. Chin-ups, for example, involve both the biceps muscles of the arms and the latissimus dorsi muscles of the back.

Antagonist Muscles

The muscle that produces the opposite movement of the prime mover is called the antagonist. For example, the triceps muscles are the antagonists of the biceps muscles. For smooth joint movements, the prime mover muscles contract and shorten as the antagonist muscles relax and lengthen. In the case of standing curls, the biceps muscles contract and shorten as the triceps muscles relax and lengthen.

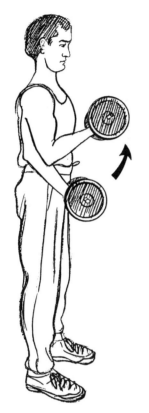 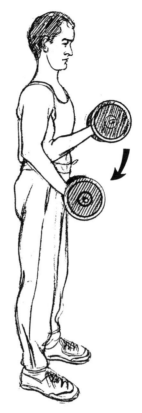 

Figure 3-4. Positive contraction of the biceps muscles, lifting an 80-pound barbell.

Figure 3-5. Negative contraction of the biceps muscles, lowering a 120-pound barbell.

Figure 3-6. Static contraction of the biceps muscles, holding a 100-pound barbell.

Stabilizer Muscles

For the desired movements to occur in certain joints, other joints must be stabilized. For example, to properly perform standing curls, the torso must remain erect and the upper arms must be held against the sides. The torso is stabilized by static contraction of the low-back muscles, and the upper arms are stabilized by static contraction of the chest and upper-back muscles.

A similar torso stabilization must occur to properly perform push-ups. The midsection muscles must contract statically to maintain the body in a straight and stable position. The muscles that perform stabilizing functions are referred to as stabilizer muscles.

MUSCLE RELAXATION

The natural state of skeletal muscle is called relaxation. Muscle fibers contract only upon receiving appropriate nerve stimulation. In the absence of nerve stimulation, the contraction mechanism is inactive, and muscle tension is not developed.

An important component of muscle relaxation is that an antagonist muscle relaxes when a prime mover muscle contracts. That is, at the same time a prime mover muscle is stimulated to contract and shorten, the antagonist muscle is cued to relax and lengthen. Actually, the degree of tension in the opposing muscle groups (prime movers and antagonists) is precisely regulated by the nervous system to produce smooth movements with varying degrees of force and speed.

MUSCLE PROTECTION

Your body is equipped with built-in mechanisms to prevent tissue damage that could result from too much muscle tension or too much muscle stretch. Receptors located within your muscle tendons respond to excessive stress by decreasing muscle contraction force, thereby preventing muscle tension to rise to dangerous levels.

Other receptors located within your muscles are sensitive to muscle stretch. Whenever a muscle is stretched too far or too quickly, these receptors trigger a reflex action that causes the muscle to contract, thereby reducing the risk of injury.

MUSCLE FATIGUE

Although the exact mechanisms responsible for muscle fatigue are not fully understood, there are many possible causes. One of these is the temporary depletion of energy sources as a muscle continues to contract forcefully. Another cause may be the accumulation of by-products, such as lactic acid, within the muscle.

Muscle fatigue may be experienced in many degrees, up to the point of temporary muscle failure. At temporary muscle failure, the muscle is no longer able to contract positively. However, after a few seconds rest, the muscle is partially recovered, and after two minutes rest, the muscle energy sources are largely replaced.

MUSCLE-JOINT MOVEMENT

The function of skeletal muscle is to produce tension that causes joint movement. Muscles are attached to bones by connective tissue called tendons. As il-

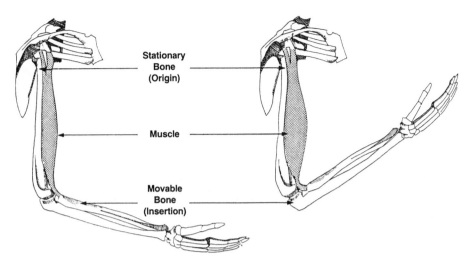

Figure 3-7. Contraction of a muscle resulting in the movement of one bone toward another. The stationary bone is referred to as the muscle origin and the movable bone as the muscle insertion.

lustrated in Figure 3-7, contraction of a skeletal muscle typically moves one bone toward another bone. Generally speaking, the bone that remains stationary is considered the muscle origin, and the bone that moves is considered the muscle insertion.

The focus of this book is muscle–joint movement. More specifically, the remaining chapters will teach you how to properly and productively exercise the muscles responsible for the joint movements in Figure 3-8.

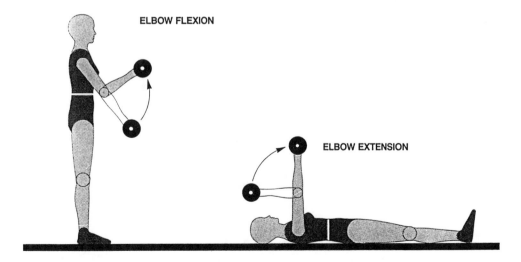

Figure 3-8. Schematic illustrations of joint movements.

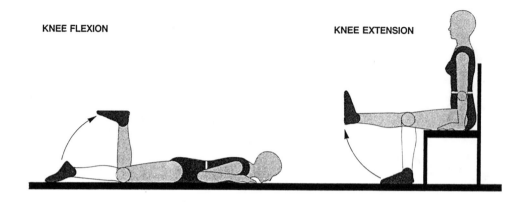

KNEE FLEXION   KNEE EXTENSION

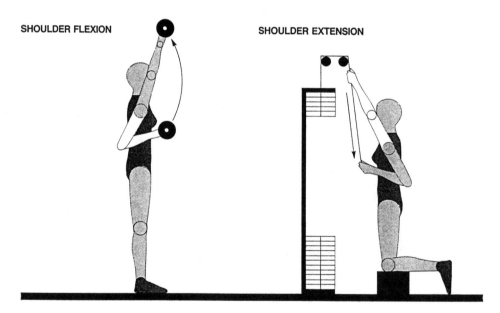

SHOULDER FLEXION   SHOULDER EXTENSION

Figure 3-8. (*continued*)

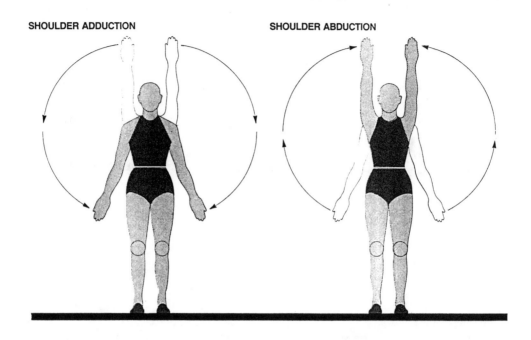

SHOULDER ADDUCTION

SHOULDER ABDUCTION

SHOULDER HORIZONTAL FLEXION

SHOULDER HORIZONTAL EXTENSION

Figure 3-8. (*continued*)

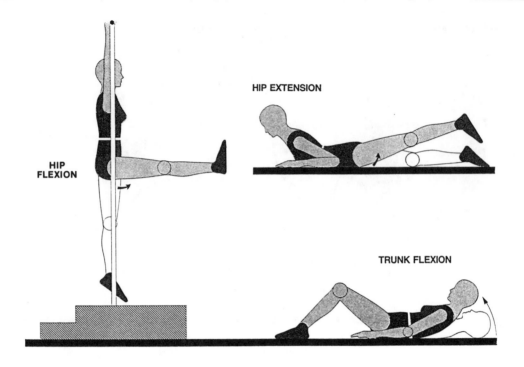

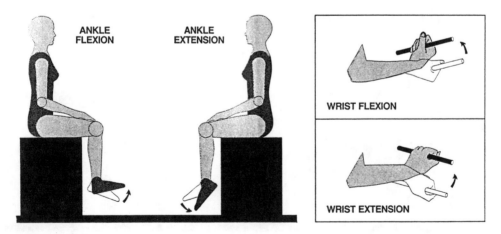

Figure 3-8. (*continued*)

4
Strength Training Performance Factors

There are a number of factors, over which you have little control, that influence your muscle strength. These include muscle size, muscle length, muscle fiber type, tendon insertion point, sex, and age. Other factors, over which you do have control, that affect your strength performance are training experience, training technique, and training specificity. It is important to address all of these factors when designing and evaluating your personal strength training program.

MUSCLE SIZE

The cross-section size of a muscle largely determines the amount of force it can produce. In general, a square centimeter of muscle tissue can produce from two to four pounds of contraction force. It therefore stands to reason that a larger muscle can exert more force than a smaller muscle.

The cross-section area of a muscle is initially determined by heredity. Consequently, a large-framed person is likely to have larger muscles than a small-framed person (see Figure 4-1). However, strength training can increase the

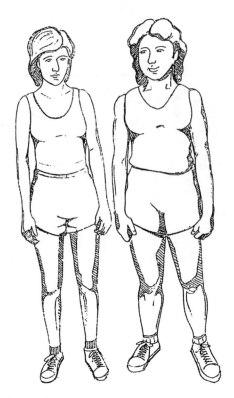

Figure 4-1. Small-framed and large-framed females of equal height.

cross-section size of muscles by enlarging the individual muscle fibers. The gradual increase in muscle size that results from strength training is called hypertrophy. Conversely, the gradual decrease in muscle size that occurs when strength training is discontinued is known as atrophy.

MUSCLE LENGTH

Your muscle length affects your muscle size. Figure 4-2 illustrates a short, medium, and long calf muscle. Generally speaking, short muscles have low size potential, medium length muscles have medium size potential, and long muscles have high size potential. Most of us inherit medium length muscles. However, everyone can improve their muscle size and strength through sensible strength training. A simple method for estimating your muscle length is presented in Chapter 8.

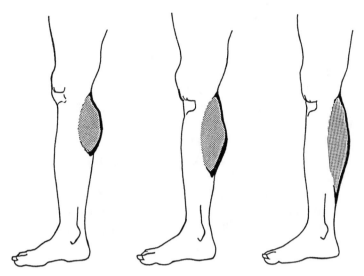

Figure 4-2. Comparison of short, medium, and long calf muscles.

MUSCLE FIBER TYPE

In addition to muscle size and muscle length, muscle fiber type is an important performance factor. Individual muscle fibers basically possess either slow-twitch or fast-twitch characteristics.

Slow-twitch muscle fibers bear the greatest burden in aerobic activities (i.e., those that require long periods of low force production). These fibers are smaller and better-suited for aerobic energy utilization. Persons who inherit a high percentage of slow-twitch muscle fibers typically excel as long distance runners, swimmers, and cyclists.

Fast-twitch muscle fibers bear the greatest burden in anaerobic activities (i.e., those that require short periods of high force production). These fibers are larger and better suited for anaerobic energy utilization. Persons who inherit a high percentage of fast-twitch muscle fibers typically excel as sprinters, jumpers, and throwers.

Individuals with mostly fast-twitch muscle fibers have greater potential for increasing muscle size and strength than individuals with mostly slow-twitch fibers. However, everyone can improve their muscle size and strength through proper strength training. A method for estimating your muscle fiber type is presented in Chapter 8.

TENDON INSERTION POINT

It is possible for two persons to produce the same amount of muscle tension but to differ considerably in the amount of weight they can lift. This is due to the fact that human movement is dependent upon a system of levers involving the bones, joints, and muscles. The bones act as levers, the joints serve as axes of rotation, and the muscles produce movement forces.

For instance, the biceps muscle attaches to the lower arm near the elbow joint (see Figure 4-3). This is called the tendon insertion point. With the elbow at a right angle, the muscle force times the force arm (distance from the elbow to the tendon insertion point) equals the resistance times the resistance arm (distance from the elbow to the dumbbell). With this in mind, consider how the point of tendon insertion can greatly influence your effective strength output.

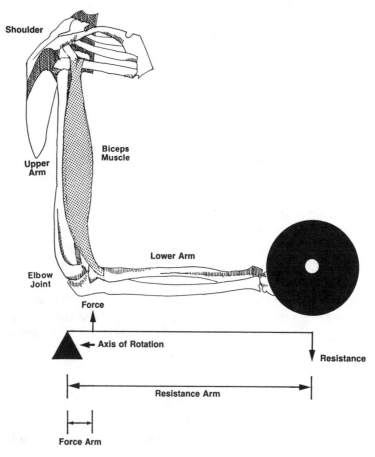

Figure 4-3. The biceps muscle attaches to the lower arm near the elbow joint. With the elbow at a right angle, the muscle force times the force arm equals the resistance times the resistance arm.

EXAMPLE ONE

Mary has a 10-inch forearm with a biceps insertion point one inch from her elbow joint. If Mary can produce 200 pounds of force in her biceps muscle, how heavy a dumbbell can she hold at a right angle?

Muscle Force × Force Arm = Resistance × Resistance Arm
200 pounds × 1 inch = 20 pounds × 10 inches
Mary can hold a 20-pound dumbbell at a right angle.

EXAMPLE TWO

Cindy also has a 10-inch forearm, but her biceps insertion point is three-quarters inch from her elbow joint. If Cindy can likewise produce 200 pounds of force in her biceps muscle, how heavy a dumbbell can she hold at a right angle?

Muscle Force × Force Arm = Resistance × Resistance Arm
200 pounds × ¾ inch = 15 pounds × 10 inches
Mary can hold a 15-pound dumbbell at a right angle.

In these examples, Mary and Cindy can both produce a maximum biceps tension of 200 pounds. However, due to a more favorable tendon insertion point, Mary can hold a heavier dumbbell (20 pounds versus 15 pounds) at a right angle.

These examples also demonstrate that human lever systems require large amounts of muscle force to overcome small amounts of resistive force. Although this is a disadvantage with respect to movement force, it is an advantage with respect to movement speed.

SEX

Regarding muscle size and strength, there are definite differences between men and women. During the adolescent growth years, males develop larger muscles than females, which provides a significant strength advantage. Furthermore, strength training increases muscle size to a greater degree in males than in females. This is due to the male sex hormone testosterone, which plays a major role in muscle growth and hypertrophy.

By virtue of their genetic makeup, males generally have greater potential for muscle size and strength than females. Nonetheless, on a pound-for-pound basis, there is little strength difference between males and females. In one research study, I evaluated the thigh strength of 900 men and women on a Nautilus leg extension machine. On the average, both men and women performed 10 repetitions with resistance equaling about 60 percent of their body weight.

Men are stronger than women due to muscle quantity, not muscle quality. Men simply have more muscle mass than women and therefore have a higher strength potential.

In terms of strength development, men and women progress at about the same rate. Several research studies have revealed strength gains between 3 and 6 percent per week for both males and females involved in similar strength training programs. Figure 4-4 illustrates the rate of strength development for male and female subjects during five weeks of strength training.

AGE

Males and females gain muscle size and strength through the process of maturation until about age 20. However, unless they engage in regular strength exercise, their muscle size and strength gradually decreases throughout adult-

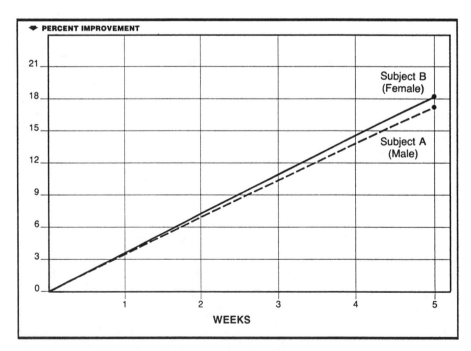

Figure 4-4. Increase in bench press strength as indicated by percent improvement (body weights: male = 160 pounds, female = 95 pounds).

hood. Fortunately, it is possible to add muscle mass at any age through progressive resistance exercise. Consider the results of a two-month strength training program on 81 children and 282 adults. As shown in Figure 4-5, the youth added four pounds of muscle, and the adults gained over three pounds of muscle.

Another study compared the rate of strength development in women under age 20 and women over age 20. The subjects under 20 years of age increased their strength by 6 percent per week. The subjects over the age of 20 increased their strength by 3 percent per week. Although the effects of resistance exercise may be enhanced during the growth years, persons of all ages can increase their muscle strength.

TRAINING EXPERIENCE

Training experience refers to the length of time you have been involved in a strength training program. Generally speaking, the person who has trained regularly for three years will make smaller strength gains than the person who has trained for only three weeks. During the early stages of a strength training program, improvement usually comes quickly due to learning processes. As you approach your strength potential, increases are smaller and less frequent.

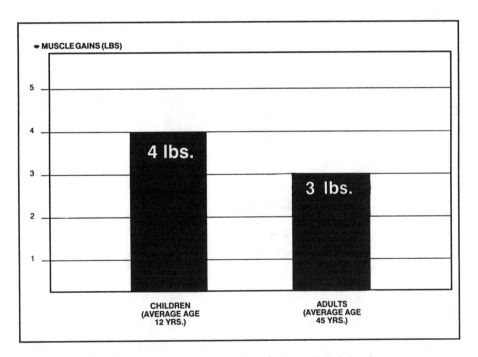

Figure 4-5. Muscle gains after two months of strength training in two age groups (363 subjects).

As illustrated in Figure 4-6, the rate of strength development may decrease considerably during the first three months of training. The 40 percent strength gain experienced during the first month may fall to a 10 percent strength gain during the second month, and to only a 2.5 percent strength gain during the third month.

Experienced strength trainers tend to encounter strength plateaus, which can be discouraging. However, with appropriate changes in your exercise routine, you can continue to make performance improvements and maintain your training motivation.

TRAINING TECHNIQUE

Your training technique may have a profound influence on both strength development and injury risk. For example, Scott can curl a 75-pound barbell when he uses a slow movement speed. This technique is characterized by consistent muscle force throughout the movement range. It provides excellent stimulus for Scott's biceps muscles and poses little risk of injury.

On the other hand, Scott can curl a 100-pound barbell when he uses a fast

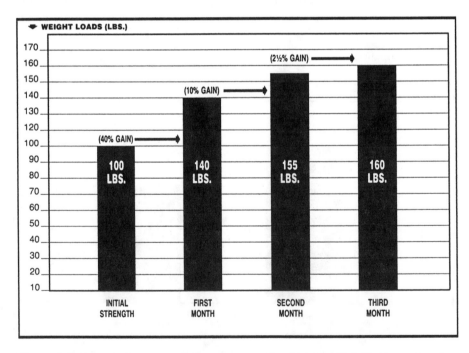

Figure 4-6. Sample three-month improvement for athlete with initial leg extension weight load of 100 pounds.

movement speed. This technique is characterized by high muscle force at the beginning of the movement range and low muscle force thereafter. It provides some stimulus for Scott's biceps muscles but carries a high risk of injury.

Fast lifting movements make use of momentum, have a high injury potential, and are not recommended. Slow lifting movements are preferred for both training safety and training effectiveness.

TRAINING SPECIFICITY

People frequently equate hard work with success, but this is only true when there is a strong relationship between the work performed and the desired outcomes. Both a one-hour run and a one-hour weight training session are hard work, but each produces a specific physical response. A serious distance runner and a serious weightlifter may train over an hour each day, but their physical appearances are very different.

Training that involves long periods of low-intensity exercise may develop cardiovascular endurance but may not improve muscle strength. Conversely,

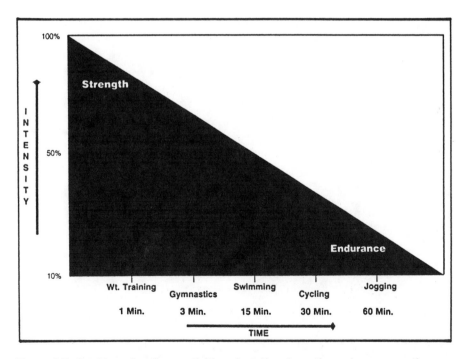

Figure 4-7. Position of various activities along the strength–endurance continuum. Note that strength-related activities are of relatively high intensity and short duration.

training that involves short periods of high-intensity exercise may develop muscle strength but may not improve cardiovascular endurance.

You should therefore train in a specific manner to obtain specific results: strength training for muscular development and endurance training for cardiovascular development. Figure 4-7 indicates the approximate positions of various physical activities along the strength–endurance continuum. Note that strength-related exercise is of high-intensity and short duration, whereas endurance-related exercise is of low-intensity and long duration.

5
Strength Training Guidelines

Twenty-five years ago, the only people who ran were competitive athletes. Today, thousands of exercise enthusiasts run to improve their cardiovascular fitness. A few years ago, the only people who lifted weights were competitive bodybuilders. Today, thousands of exercise enthusiasts lift weights to improve their muscular fitness.

Unfortunately, many exercisers work too long and too hard to achieve their strength goals. Just as it is not necessary to run two hours a day to develop cardiovascular fitness, it is not necessary to lift weights two hours a day to develop muscular fitness. Research clearly indicates that you can attain excellent strength results by training 30 minutes a day, three days a week.

Consider the physical changes experienced by Scott Enos, a muscular weight trainer who performed about three hours of strength exercise six days a week. Although there is nothing wrong with strength training almost 18 hours each week, I believed that Scott could achieve the same results with much less exercise. Scott agreed to exercise under my supervision for 20 minutes a day, three days a week, in a high-intensity manner. That is, he trained very hard with little rest between exercises. After eight weeks (eight hours) of high-intensity strength training, Scott added six pounds of muscle.

Scott's excellent results showed that brief strength training sessions can be very productive. But would they work for people who exercise with less intensity?

To answer that question, I conducted research studies with youth (81 boys and girls) and adults (282 men and women). All of the subjects trained at a moderate intensity, 20 minutes a day, three days a week. After eight weeks (eight hours) of moderate-intensity strength training, the youth gained four pounds of muscle, and the adults added three pounds of muscle.

Although better results may have been possible with longer or harder training, the brief exercise sessions were certainly effective. This is important information for busy individuals who have limited time for strength training.

During the past few years there has been a definite trend towards safe and efficient strength training programs. Three national exercise associations, the YMCA of the USA, the American Council on Exercise, and the American College of Sports Medicine, have recently issued guidelines for sensible strength training. The three sets of guidelines are consistent in their recommendations for exercise selection, sets, repetitions, intensity, progression, speed, range, and frequency.

The guidelines are not intended to exclude other strength training programs nor to represent the more specialized workouts performed by competitive bodybuilders and weightlifters. However, they are ideal for persons who want to attain higher levels of strength fitness in a safe and efficient manner. I encourage you to apply these guidelines to your own strength training program.

EXERCISE SELECTION

The guidelines advise you to perform about 10 exercises for the major muscle groups of the body. Training all of your major muscle groups assures balanced muscular development. The national YMCA textbook, *Building Strength at the YMCA*, identifies the following major muscle groups: front thigh (quadriceps), rear thigh (hamstrings), lower back, abdominals, chest, upper back, shoulders, biceps, triceps, and neck. Other important muscle groups include the inner thighs (hip adductors), outer thighs (hip abductors), calves, shins, forearm flexors, forearm extensors, and sides (left and right obliques).

While it is essential to train opposing muscle groups, the exercise resistance may be different. For example, the quadriceps muscles are much stronger than the hamstring muscles at the knee joint. Therefore you would normally use more resistance in a quadriceps exercise (leg extensions) than in a hamstring exercise (leg curls).

Practical Application

A sound strength training program should include exercises for all of your major muscle groups. Proper exercise selection provides balanced muscle development, sets a firm foundation for further improvement, and reduces the risk of overuse injuries.

It is also advisable to train your opposing muscle groups in pairs, such as the biceps and triceps. I prefer beginning with the larger muscles of the legs and progressing to the smaller muscles of the midsection, torso, arms, and neck.

EXERCISE SETS

The guidelines call for one set of strength exercise for each of the major muscle groups. Although more sets may be performed if desired, research indicates that excellent results can be obtained with single-set strength training. The following two studies clearly show that one set of strength exercise is an effective means for strength development.

The first study compared training with one or two sets of exercise on Nautilus equipment. Twenty-two men and women performed one set of each exercise, and 22 other men and women completed two sets of each exercise. As illustrated in Figure 5-1, all of the subjects made excellent strength gains during the course of the study. However, there were no significant differences in strength development between the subjects who performed one set of each exercise and the subjects who completed two sets of each exercise.

The second study compared training with one, two, or three sets of chin-ups and bar-dips on a Gravitron machine. Seventy-seven adults were tested for the

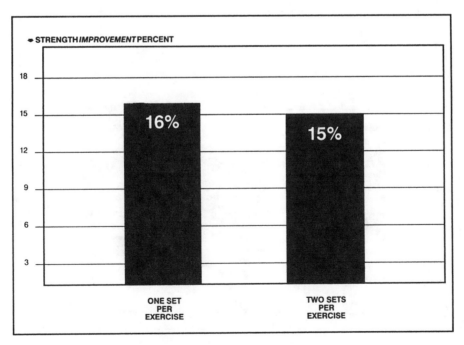

Figure 5-1. Comparison of one-set and two-set strength training (44 subjects).

total number of chin-ups and bar-dips they could complete before and after the 10-week training period. As shown in Figure 5-2, all three training groups improved their chin-up and bar-dip performance. However, there were no significant differences in strength development among the subjects who performed one set of each exercise, the subjects who did two sets of each exercise, and the subjects who completed three sets of each exercise.

Practical Application

Based on the results of these studies, it appears that the number of training sets you perform may be a matter of personal preference. It seems that the essential stimulus for basic strength development is one hard set of exercise.

With respect to training effectiveness, I do not favor one-set, two-set, or three-set training, as all seem to be equally beneficial. However, with respect to training efficiency, I prefer single-set training because it produces similar strength results with less exercise time.

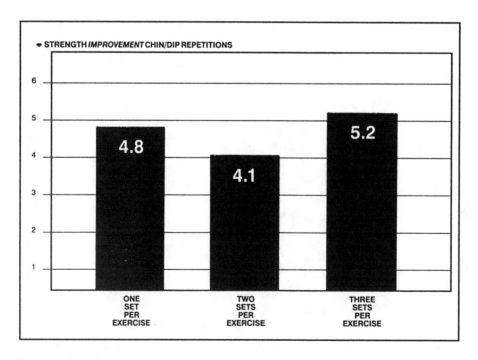

Figure 5-2. Comparison of one-, two-, and three-set strength training (77 subjects).

EXERCISE REPETITIONS

The guidelines recommend eight to 12 repetitions as the best training range to develop muscle strength and endurance. Research indicates that most people can complete between eight and 12 repetitions with about 75 percent of their maximum resistance.

A study of 87 men and women first determined the maximum resistance each subject could perform one time. The subjects were then tested for the number of repetitions they could complete with 75 percent of their maximum resistance.

As illustrated in Figure 5-3, most of the subjects (62 out of 87) completed between eight and 13 repetitions with 75 percent of their maximum resistance. It is assumed that these individuals have an even mix of fast-twitch (low endurance) and slow-twitch (high endurance) muscle fibers.

Nine of the subjects performed fewer than eight repetitions. Because all of these individuals were successful power athletes, it is assumed that they have predominantly fast-twitch (low endurance) muscle fibers.

Twelve of the subjects performed more than 13 repetitions. Because all of these individuals were outstanding endurance athletes, it is assumed that they have predominantly slow-twitch (high endurance) muscle fibers.

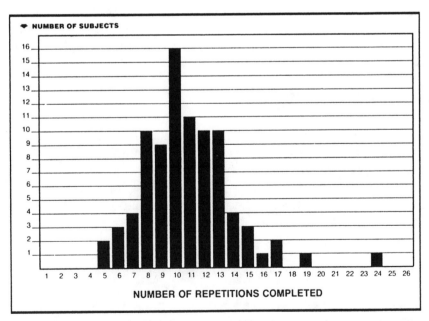

Figure 5-3. Distribution of repetitions completed with 75 percent of maximum weight load (87 subjects).

Practical Application

This research indicates that most people can complete between eight and 13 repetitions with 75 percent of their maximum resistance. In my opinion, these individuals should typically train with about eight to 12 repetitions per set of exercise. Persons with predominantly fast-twitch (low endurance) muscle fibers should probably train with fewer (four to eight) repetitions per set. Persons with predominantly slow-twitch (high endurance) muscle fibers should probably train with more (12-16) repetitions per set. A method for estimating your muscle fiber type is presented in Chapter 8.

EXERCISE INTENSITY

According to the American College of Sports Medicine, any amount of overload results in some strength development, but higher intensity effort produces a greater effect. The guidelines recommend training to near muscle fatigue with each exercise set. Near muscle fatigue generally means working to the point where you can no longer lift the resistance (temporary muscle failure).

Practical Application

Quite simply, working at a higher exercise intensity produces better strength results. Assuming that you train with eight to 12 repetitions per set, be sure the resistance is heavy enough to fatigue your muscles within that repetition range. It is important to keep working until your muscles can no longer lift the resistance.

EXERCISE PROGRESSION

The key to strength development is progressive resistance exercise. In order to build stronger muscles you must gradually add more resistance to your training exercises. When you work your muscles a little harder than usual, they respond positively and become stronger. However, when you work your muscles a lot harder than usual, they respond negatively and become weaker or injured.

It is therefore important to plan your exercise progression in a systematic manner. I prefer a double progressive system, in which you alternately increase repetitions and resistance. Let's say that you can perform eight curls with 50 pounds. Continue training with 50 pounds until you can complete 12 curls, then increase the resistance to 52.5 pounds. The additional resistance will reduce the number of repetitions you can perform. When you can complete 12 repetitions with 52.5 pounds, increase the resistance to 55 pounds. Continue training in this manner.

Practical Application

Although there are many ways to increase your exercise resistance, it is important to do so in a progressive manner. My recommendation is to increase the resistance by a small amount whenever you can complete 12 repetitions. As a rule, the exercise resistance should not be increased by more than 5 percent per session.

EXERCISE SPEED

The guidelines call for strength exercise to be performed at a moderate to slow speed. This is because slow movements permit a more consistent application of force and provide a lower risk of injury. Consider the following four reasons for performing strength exercise in a slow and controlled manner.

1. More Muscle Tension: Slow strength training produces a longer period of muscle tension than fast strength training. In Figure 5-4, muscle tension is represented by the area of the force curves. You will note that as the movement speed increases, the muscle tension decreases. Because muscle tension is an important factor in strength development, slow movement speeds are recommended.

2. More Muscle Force: Slow strength training produces a higher level of muscle force than fast strength training. In Figure 5-4, muscle force is represented by the height of the force curves. You will observe that as the movement speed increases, the muscle force decreases. Because muscle force is an important factor in strength development, slow movement speeds are recommended.

3. Less Tissue Trauma: Speed is an essential ingredient in many athletic events. However, these events are typically performed with body weight (high jump) or with a light implement (tennis racquet). Performing heavy resistance strength exercise at a fast speed places high stress on your muscles and connec-

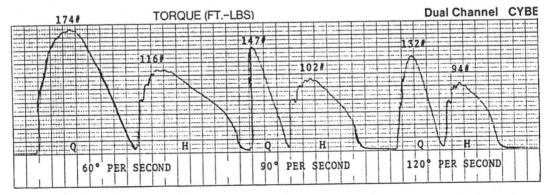

Figure 5-4. Isokinetic assessment of muscle force production at various movement speeds.

tive tissue. Because slow movement speeds cause less tissue trauma and have a lower injury potential, they are recommended for strength exercise.

4. Less Momentum: Momentum plays a role in virtually all weight training exercises. The faster the lifting movement, the greater the momentum. As the momentum component increases, the muscle component decreases. An example of momentum-assisted weight training is bouncing the barbell off your chest during the bench press exercise. In addition to the higher injury potential, this careless use of momentum reduces the training effect on the target muscle groups. Because slow movement speeds involve less momentum, they are recommended for strength exercise.

Practical Application

Slow lifting speeds are characterized by more muscle tension, more muscle force, less tissue trauma, and less momentum. For these reasons it is recommended that strength exercises be performed in a slow and controlled manner. More specifically, I suggest that you take about two seconds for each lifting movement and at least as long for each lowering movement.

EXERCISE RANGE

The guidelines recommend that each exercise be performed through a full range of movement. This strengthens the muscle at all joint positions and maintains joint flexibility. It is particularly useful to emphasize the fully contracted position of each exercise movement. First, the fully contracted position provides an excellent stimulus for strength development. Second, the fully contracted position assures that the opposing muscle group is fully stretched. For example, at the end point of a biceps curl, the biceps muscles are fully contracted and the opposing triceps muscles are fully stretched.

Movement range should be taken into consideration when selecting your strength exercises. Other things being equal, the longer the movement range, the more work performed. For example, chin-ups performed with a narrow grip provide a greater movement range than chin-ups performed with a wide grip.

Practical Application

It is recommended that strength exercise be performed slowly through a full range of movement. You should try to attain a fully contracted position on each repetition. Remember that you only increase strength in the positions that you exercise.

EXERCISE FREQUENCY

The guidelines recommend a minimum of two training sessions per week for strength development. However, research indicates that three training sessions per week produce even better strength gains. Training every day is not advisable because your muscles require about 48 hours recovery and building time between workouts.

As illustrated in Figure 5-5, muscle strength decreases during a workout, then gradually builds to a slightly higher level of strength during the recovery period. For best results, you should take each workout at the peak of your building cycle. If the exercise resistance feels a little lighter each workout, then your exercise frequency is appropriate.

Although bodybuilders generally train six days a week, they exercise different muscle groups on different days. For example, they may train their legs on Mondays, Wednesdays, and Fridays, and exercise their upper body muscles on Tuesdays, Thursdays, and Saturdays.

Practical Application

For a basic strength training program, I recommend three exercise sessions per week. It is a good practice to exercise all of your major muscle groups each

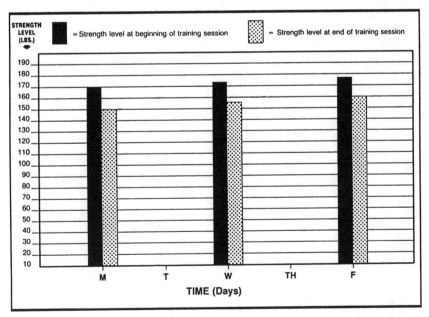

Figure 5-5. Hypothetical pattern of muscle response when recovery period is appropriate with respect to training intensity. When sufficient rest is obtained between training sessions, the muscle rebuilds to a slightly higher level of strength.

training day and to rest all of your major muscle groups each non-training day. If you are unable to follow an every-other-day training schedule, an every-third-day exercise routine will produce nearly the same results.

EXERCISE BREATHING

Although not an official guideline, it is important to breathe properly when performing strength exercise. Holding your breath during forceful muscular effort is a dangerous practice. The internal pressure created by breath-holding coupled with the external pressure of tightly contracted muscles is sufficient to restrict blood flow and elevate blood pressure. Consequently, you should breathe continuously during every set of strength exercise.

Practical Application

The preferred breathing pattern is to inhale during lowering movements and to exhale during lifting movements. In this manner, air pressure decreases as muscular pressure increases, and vice versa. However, as long as you breathe regularly and do not hold your breath, you should not encounter any problems.

SUMMARY OF STRENGTH TRAINING GUIDELINES

The following summarizes the exercise guidelines recommended for a safe and productive strength training experience.

Selection: You should perform at least one exercise for each of your major muscle groups.

Major Muscle Group	Sample Exercise
Quadriceps	Leg extension machine
Hamstrings	Leg curl machine
Lower back	Low-back machine
Abdominals	Abdominal machine
Chest	10-degree chest machine
Upper back	Pullover machine
Shoulders	Lateral raise machine
Biceps	Biceps curl machine
Triceps	Triceps extension machine
Neck flexors/extensors	Neck machine

Sets: You may perform one, two, or three sets of each exercise depending upon your personal preference. Single-set training produces similar strength benefits and requires less exercise time.

Repetitions: Because most people can complete eight to 12 repetitions with 75 percent of their maximum resistance, this is the recommended repetition range under most circumstances.

Intensity: You should continue each exercise until you can no longer lift the resistance. This should normally occur between eight and 12 repetitions when using an appropriate resistance.

Progression: A good rule of exercise progression is to increase your training resistance by about 5 percent whenever you can complete 12 repetitions.

Speed: It is advisable to perform your strength exercise in a slow and controlled manner, taking about two seconds for each lifting movement and at least as long for each lowering movement.

Range: Whenever possible, you should perform your strength exercise through a full range of movement. This provides more strengthening benefit to the target muscle group and more stretching benefit to the opposing muscle group.

Frequency: I recommend an every-other-day strength training schedule to provide sufficient muscle building time between workouts. If this is not possible, an every-third-day exercise program will produce almost the same results.

Breathing: Never hold your breath when performing strength exercise. Do your best to exhale during the lifting movements and to inhale during the lowering movements.

6
Equipment Selection and Safety

The key to strength development is progressive resistance. That is, to gain more strength, you must use more resistance. Because body weight exercises such as push-ups and sit-ups use more repetitions rather than more resistance, they are less effective for building muscle strength.

Progressive resistance can be provided in many forms, including weights, air pressure, hydraulic pressure, and electrical resistance. Although the type of resistance may be different, the strength training principles are exactly the same. The results may vary somewhat, however, based on the type of equipment utilized.

DYNAMIC EXERCISE

Strength training performed with weights (free weights or weight-stack machines) provides dynamic exercise. In this type of exercise, the resistance force determines your muscle force. The more resistance you use, the more muscle force you produce; the less resistance you use, the less muscle force you produce. Dynamic exercise offers resistance during both the positive and negative phase of the exercise movement.

Strength training performed with dumbbells or barbells is referred to as *dynamic constant resistance exercise* because the weight load does not change during the exercise movement. Strength training performed with certain weight-stack machines is referred to as *dynamic variable resistance exercise* because the weight load changes automatically during the exercise movement. This is typically accomplished by means of levers or cams designed to vary the resistance in accordance with your muscle strength. That is, you receive less resistance in weaker muscle positions and more resistance in stronger muscle positions.

Free Weights and Weight-Stack Machines

Although most strength training participants perform dynamic exercises, some prefer free weights while others opt for weight-stack machines. Both free weights and weight-stack machines provide visual feedback, which serves as an excellent source of motivation. Most of us like to see tangible evidence of our exercise efforts and having to add weight plates clearly indicates performance progress.

Free weights may be advantageous in terms of cost, convenience, and exercise variety. Barbell and dumbbell exercises also involve the use of stabilizer muscles to provide necessary balance and control.

Weight-stack machines may be advantageous in terms of exercise safety, muscle isolation, and resistance factors. Many weight-stack machines provide supportive structure, rotary movement, direct resistance, and variable resistance. Let's examine a common free-weight exercise, dumbbell flies, and a representative machine exercise, the 10-degree chest, with respect to these four training factors.

1. Supportive Structure: Supportive structure is important for safety purposes, particularly concerning the lower back. As illustrated in Figures 6-1 and 6-2, both dumbbell flies and the 10-degree chest provide support for the lower back. Some exercisers place their feet on the bench to flatten the lower back while others keep their feet on the floor to enhance stability. In either case, it is essential to keep the hips on the bench throughout the exercise.

2. Rotary Movement: Basically, an exercise movement is either linear (straight) or rotary (curved). Linear movements involve two or more joints, whereas rotary movements involve a single joint action. Rotary movements are therefore advantageous for isolating specific muscle groups. Both dumbbell flies and the 10-degree chest produce rotary movement of the arms around the shoulder joint. This action emphasizes the chest muscles, with some assistance from the front shoulder muscles (see Figures 6-1 and 6-2).

3. Direct Resistance: Direct resistance is another means for isolating specific muscle groups. Because dumbbell flies require you to grip the resistance, the forearm and upper arm muscles are actively involved in this exercise. When these muscles fatigue, you must stop the exercise, even though the chest mus-

Figure 6-1. Supported dumbbell fly.

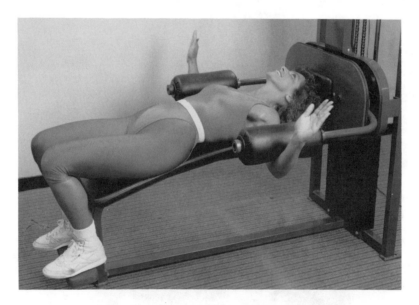

Figure 6-2. Supported 10-degree chest exercise.

cles may not have worked to capacity. The 10-degree chest requires the resistance pads be placed directly against the arms, to which the chest muscles attach. With direct resistance, the forearm and upper arm muscles are bypassed, and the exercise may be continued until the chest muscles are fatigued (see Figures 6-1 and 6-2).

4. Variable Resistance: Due to leverage factors, the first phase of the dumbbell fly places your chest muscles in a weaker position. Conversely, the last phase places your chest muscles in a stronger position. Because the dumbbell resistance remains about the same, the resistance force is not well-matched to your muscle force throughout the exercise movement. As a result, dumbbell flies have a rather high injury potential and a rather low strength building potential.

The 10-degree chest attempts to compensate for the leverage changes with a counter leverage system. As illustrated in Figure 6-3, an oval cam and chain arrangement automatically changes the resistance throughout the movement. Because the first phase of the 10-degree chest exercise places your chest muscles in a weaker position, the cam provides a lower resistance. Because the last phase places your chest muscles in a stronger position, the cam provides a higher resistance. In this manner, the resistance force is well-matched to your muscle force throughout the exercise movement. Due to variable resistance, the 10-degree chest has a rather low injury potential and a rather high strength building potential.

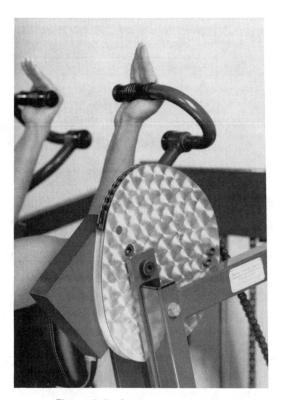

Figure 6-3. Oval cam and chain.

EQUIPMENT COMPARISON

Table 6-1 provides comparative information on several types of popular strength training equipment. Although the equipment may differ somewhat in terms of safety, effectiveness, efficiency, and expense, all are useful for increasing muscle size and strength as long as the basic training principles are applied. Regardless of the equipment used, however, injury prevention and muscle development are directly related to the strength training guidelines presented in Chapter 5.

SPACE

Be aware of space limitations when performing strength exercise. Few things present a greater safety threat than too little training space, especially if you are

Table 6-1. Comparative chart of various types of strength training equipment.

Features	Barbell type	Universal gym type	Nautilus type	Hydraulic type	Compressed air type	Computerized type
Safety features	No	Yes	Yes	Yes	Yes	Yes
Durability	Yes	Yes	Yes	Yes	Yes	Too new to determine
Concentric conractions	Yes	Yes	Yes	Yes	Yes	Yes
Eccentric contractions	Yes	Yes	Yes	No	Yes	Some yes Some no
Static contractions	Yes	Yes	Yes	No	Yes	Some yes Some no
Rotary movement (all major muscles)	No	Some yes Some no	Yes	Yes	Yes	No
Direct resistance (all major muscles)	No	Some yes Some no	Yes	Yes	Yes	No
Variable resistance (all major muscles)	No	No	Yes	Yes	Yes	Yes
Observable resistance	Yes	Yes	Yes	No	No	No

exercising with other people. Whether you train at home or in a fitness center, make sure that there is ample space to perform each exercise without interference or restrictions.

SPOTTERS

Another important safety consideration is the use of spotters for certain barbell exercises such as squats, bench presses, and incline presses. In each of these exercises, failure to raise the barbell from the bottom position may lead to serious injury. It is therefore essential to train with a spotter when performing these exercises. The spotter should give you plenty of space to perform the exercise movement but be ready to help the moment assistance is required.

In the squat, the spotter should stand behind you and move up and down in tandem. If your upward movement stalls out, the spotter should wrap his arms around your chest and help you to a standing position. In the bench press and incline press, the spotter may assist you in removing and replacing the barbell to the standards. If you need assistance to complete the pressing movement, the spotter should grasp the barbell firmly and help you lift it onto the standards.

Spotters are excellent sources of encouragement and essential for most high-intensity training techniques. Whenever possible, it is advisable to train with a competent and caring spotter.

TRAINING TECHNIQUE

Perhaps the most important safety consideration is training technique. Undoubtedly, improper exercise technique is responsible for more strength training injuries than all other causes combined. Most strength training injuries result from too much weight, too much speed, and too little support.

When too much weight is used for the target muscles to handle, additional muscle groups are utilized to produce momentum. Momentum-assisted weightlifting is a dangerous procedure because it subjects the muscles and connective tissue to high stress levels.

Too much speed has a similar effect on muscle and connective tissue. Fast exercise speeds require excessive force at the beginning of each lifting movement, thereby increasing the risk of injury.

Too little support is a frequent cause of low-back injuries. This is especially true when trying to lift too much weight overhead in an unsupported barbell press. As illustrated in Figures 6-4 and 6-5, unsupported pressing movements place considerably more stress on the low-back area than supported pressing movements.

Proper training technique is beneficial for increasing muscle strength and decreasing injury risk. Make it a priority to exercise with appropriate weight loads, controlled speeds, and supportive structures whenever possible.

Figure 6-4. Unsupported overhead press.

Figure 6-5. Supported overhead press.

7

Strength Training Concerns and Considerations

The preceding chapters have presented essential information on strength training and muscle development. At this point you should have a solid under-standing of strength fitness, both in principle and practical application. Nonethe-less, there are some relevant topics that have not been covered in the text and others that deserve additional attention. This chapter provides useful informa-tion in the following areas: (1) nutrition, (2) body composition, (3) muscle strength and endurance, (4) joint flexibility, (5) warm-ups and cool-downs, (6) female re-sponse, (7) over-30 response, (8) progress and assessment, (9) strength pla-teaus, and (10) speed and power.

DOES STRENGTH TRAINING REQUIRE A SPECIAL DIET?

The most common questions asked by strength exercisers pertain to how much protein they need for better muscular development. This is a valid concern because proteins are partly responsible for the increased size and strength of trained muscle fibers.

While few people question the importance of protein in the diet, there is considerable disagreement over the amount of protein strength trainers should consume. The recommended daily protein requirement for adults is one gram for every two pounds of body weight. That is, an adult who weighs 180 pounds should consume about 90 grams of protein per day. This is approximately three ounces of protein, which most Americans easily obtain by following a normal, balanced diet. Persons who need to increase their protein intake can do so simply by eating more protein-rich foods such as low-fat dairy products and low-fat meats.

Extra protein is not generally utilized by the body and may be harmful to your kidneys. Even when you are involved in regular strength training you do not require additional protein if your daily diet is sound. This is due to the fact that your tissue (muscle) building processes occur at a relatively constant rate and are not accelerated by the presence of additional protein. Consequently, excellent muscle development may be attained without protein supplementation if you adhere to sensible nutritional guidelines.

A desirable diet provides the proteins, carbohydrates, fats, vitamins, minerals, and water necessary for good health, and is comprised of food from the following categories.

Category 1: Meat-Poultry-Fish-Protein Foods

It is recommended that you obtain at least two servings per day of foods with a high protein content, such as:

Beans
Beef (lean)
Chicken
Egg whites
Fish
Lamb (lean)
Nuts (sparingly, due to high fat content)
Peanuts (sparingly, due to high fat content)
Pork (lean)
Shellfish
Soybeans or tofu (sparingly, due to high fat content)
Turkey

It is important to obtain all of the amino acids that are essential for protein synthesis. There are at least 10 that cannot be manufactured in your body and must be included in your diet. Although meat, eggs, and milk products supply all of the essential amino acids, no single vegetable, fruit, grain, or nut does so. Consequently, vegetarians must eat a variety of vegetables, fruits, grains, and nuts to ensure that none of the essential amino acids are excluded from their diet.

Category 2: Dairy Products

In addition to the protein sources presented in Category 1, it is recommended that you obtain two or more servings of dairy products on a daily basis. The following dairy products are excellent sources for protein and calcium, an essential nutrient for muscle contraction and bone formation.

Cheese (hard)
Cottage cheese (low-fat)
Ice milk
Milk (low-fat)
Yogurt (low-fat)

There has been considerable disagreement regarding the use of dairy products when training for muscular strength and definition. The major concern is over the high-fat content of whole-milk products. Because low-fat dairy products are readily available in nearly all grocery stores, there does not seem to be any good reason, other than allergic reactions, to avoid this highly nutritious food source. For example, 1-percent milk supplies the same amount of protein and calcium as whole milk but has far less fat and fewer calories. It is interesting to note that the principal ingredient in most high-protein supplements is non-fat dried milk.

Category 3: Fruits and Vegetables

Fruits and vegetables should make up a large percentage of your daily food intake. It is recommended that you consume at least four servings from this food group each day. All sorts of fruits and vegetables are included in this category.

Apples	Cauliflower	Onions
Asparagus	Celery	Peaches
Bananas	Cherries	Pears
Beans	Citrus fruits	Peas
Beets	Corn	Peppers
Berries	Dried fruits	Plums
Broccoli	Grapes	Potatoes
Cabbage	Lettuce	Squash
Carrots	Melons	Sweet potatoes
		Tomatoes

Fruits and vegetables are excellent sources of the carbohydrates, vitamins, and minerals that are necessary for physical health and peak performance.

Category 4: Cereals and Grains

Many Americans eat too few cereals and grains because they mistakenly believe that these foods are high in fat. Actually, most of the foods in this category (cereal, bread, pasta) have very little fat. Instead, they serve as excellent sources of complex carbohydrates, vitamins, and minerals, and reasonably good sources of protein.

Biscuits	Pancakes
Bran cereals	Pasta
Bread	Pastries
Corn cereals	Rice
Crackers	Rice cereals
Flour	Rolls
Muffins	Wheat cereals
Oat cereals	Wheat germ

Obviously, foods made from grains may vary greatly in nutrition and calorie value. For example, cereals, breads, and pasta are preferable to cakes, cookies, and pies. Many cereals and grains have the additional advantage of providing fiber, which is essential for the efficient functioning of your digestive system.

Sample Diet For Bodybuilders

Bodybuilders require a balanced diet and should follow the basic nutritional guidelines presented in the previous section. However, most competitive bodybuilders prefer to eat more protein and less fat than recommended. Without deviating too far from a sound diet, consider the following example for a bodybuilder's daily food intake.

Breakfast:	Whole wheat bread with jelly
	Wheat germ with raisins
	Low-fat milk
	Low-fat yogurt with fruit
	Orange juice
Lunch:	Tuna packed in water
	Tossed salad with oil and vinegar
	Low-fat milk
	Apple
	Banana

Dinner:	Broiled fish with lemon
	Whole grain rice
	Sweet potatoes
	Peas
	Whole wheat rolls
	Fresh fruit salad
	Vegetable juice
	Low-fat milk
	Walnut-stuffed dates
Snacks:	Low-fat yogurt
	Low-fat milk
	Fresh fruit
	Raisins, dates, and dried fruit

The sample menu is presented simply as a guideline for obtaining sound nutrition while emphasizing protein content and restricting fat intake. Of course, chicken, turkey, lean beef, or veal could be substituted for fish; and a wide variety of fruits, vegetables, grains, and low-fat dairy products could be interchanged without disrupting the basic bodybuilder's diet.

HOW DOES STRENGTH TRAINING AFFECT BODY COMPOSITION?

Few people understand the relationship between muscle and fat, particularly with respect to strength training. It is often said that when strength training is discontinued, your muscle turns into fat. This sometimes appears to happen but it is not really possible. Muscle is a tissue that tends to become bigger when it is used (hypertrophy) and smaller when it is not used (atrophy). Fat is a substance that accumulates in various parts of your body when your calorie intake exceeds your energy output. Muscles cannot physically turn into fat.

If you discontinue your strength training program and continue to eat the same number of calories, your muscles become smaller while your fat stores become larger. Consequently, your muscles appear to be replaced by fat. This situation can be avoided by adjusting your eating behavior to your activity level. That is, if you cut back both your strength training and your calorie intake, you will experience a gradual muscle loss but you will not become fat.

Actually, strength training is the best activity for enhancing your body composition because it enables you to lose fat and gain muscle at the same time. Although aerobic exercise, such as running and cycling, uses calories, it does not increase your muscle mass. Aerobic activities have a single reducing effect because calories are burned only during the exercise session.

On the other hand, strength training uses calories and increases muscle mass. Because more muscle mass requires more energy, strength training has a double reducing effect. That is, strength training burns calories during the exercise session and during non-exercise time due to the higher energy requirements of larger muscles.

This is not to suggest that aerobic activities are less important, because aerobic conditioning is fundamental to physical fitness. However, you may recall the research study from Chapter 2 in which 22 subjects performed only endurance exercise, and 50 subjects performed both endurance and strength exercise. Those who did only endurance exercise lost four pounds of fat. Those who did both endurance and strength exercise lost 10 pounds of fat and gained two pounds of muscle, for a 12-pound improvement in their body composition.

Clearly, strength training can have a positive influence on your body composition. For best results, I recommend a combination of sound diet, regular endurance exercise, and sensible strength training.

DOES MUSCLE STRENGTH AFFECT MUSCLE ENDURANCE?

As discussed in Chapter 5, some people have low endurance muscles and others have high endurance muscles. However, there is a direct relationship between muscle strength and muscle endurance. When you improve muscle strength, you automatically improve muscle endurance.

Let's say that you can perform one bench press with 100 pounds (muscle strength) and 20 repetitions with 50 pounds (muscle endurance). After 10 weeks of low repetition strength training you can perform one bench press with 150 pounds (muscle strength) and 35 repetitions with 50 pounds (muscle endurance). You are able to complete more repetitions with 50 pounds because it is now a smaller percentage of your maximum strength.

From a practical perspective, it is not necessary to train for both muscle strength and muscle endurance because these abilities are closely related. In a recent research study, 20 women trained their left leg with 10 repetitions and their right leg with 20 repetitions. After eight weeks of training, both legs made almost identical improvements in muscle strength and muscle endurance (see Table 7-1).

Proper strength training increases muscle strength and muscle endurance at the same time. As you become stronger, you can complete more repetitions with any given resistance.

Table 7-1. Effects of 10-repetition and 20-repetition training on muscle strength and muscle endurance (20 subjects).

	Muscle strength			Muscle endurance		
	Before	After	Diff.	Before	After	Diff.
10-repetition training	52 lbs.	60 lbs.	8 lbs.	10 reps	17 reps	7 reps
20-repetition training	52 lbs.	60 lbs.	8 lbs.	11 reps	18 reps	7 reps

HOW DOES STRENGTH TRAINING AFFECT JOINT FLEXIBILITY?

Flexibility refers to the range of motion in a joint and is related to both injury prevention and force production. Tight joints increase the risk of injury and decrease the distance over which force can be applied. Consequently, a golfer who increases his shoulder joint flexibility will reduce his risk of injury and increase his driving distance, if other factors remain the same.

The key to joint flexibility is muscle stretchability, which is best accomplished through full-range movements. Strength exercise can be an effective means for improving joint flexibility when performed in an appropriate manner. For example, in the fully contracted position of the biceps curl, the opposing triceps muscles are fully stretched. Likewise, in the fully contracted position of the triceps extension, the opposing biceps muscles are fully stretched. Consequently, if you strengthen all of your major muscle groups through a full range of movement, you will also stretch them.

It should be understood that a high level of muscle strength does not preclude a high level of joint flexibility. A well-designed and properly executed strength training program is useful for developing both muscle strength and joint flexibility.

HOW IMPORTANT ARE WARM-UPS AND COOL-DOWNS?

It is generally agreed that a few minutes of warm-up activity may be beneficial concerning injury prevention and athletic performance. A basic warm-up includes some light aerobic exercise (walking, jogging, stationary cycling) and some slow stretching movements for your major muscle groups.

Activities that require precise movements benefit from a specific warm-up in the form of progressively more forceful trials. For example, baseball pitchers, football quarterbacks, and shot putters warm up with a few easy throws, then gradually increase their intensity until they are throwing at full effort. In like manner, competitive weightlifters typically perform progressively heavier warm-up sets before attempting maximum weight loads.

On the other hand, if you train with eight to 12 repetitions per set, it may not be necessary to perform preliminary sets with lighter weights. A weight load that you can lift for eight to 12 repetitions is approximately 75 percent of your maximum resistance and should not cause injury or require special preparation. Also, when training in a slow and controlled manner, it takes about 60-90 seconds to complete eight to 12 repetitions. Consequently, the target muscles experience a specific warm-up prior to the most difficult repetitions.

Although more attention is usually given to the warm-up, the cool-down that follows your workout is very important. The primary purpose of the cool-down is to return blood to your heart. When you stop exercising, blood accumulates in your legs, placing considerable stress on your heart and circulatory system. By continuing to exercise at a lower level, the muscle contractions assist blood flow and permit a gradual return to resting circulation.

The cool-down is essentially a warm-up in reverse, involving some light aerobic activity and stretching exercises. In a very real sense, the cool-down may mean the difference between leaving your workout feeling exhausted or feeling invigorated.

HOW DO WOMEN RESPOND TO STRENGTH TRAINING?

The average American woman is about four inches shorter and 30 pounds lighter than the average American man. In addition, she has approximately 15 pounds more fat weight and 45 pounds less lean weight. It is therefore not surprising that the average female is weaker than the average male. In fact, men typically use 50-100 percent more resistance in their strength training exercises.

However, women may be almost as strong as men on a pound-for-pound basis. Observations of almost 900 exercisers revealed that the average male could perform 10 leg extensions with a resistance equaling just over 60 percent of his body weight, and the average female could complete 10 leg extensions with a resistance equaling just under 60 percent of her body weight.

Due to genetic factors and lower levels of testosterone, few women have the potential to develop large muscles. However, most women can improve their muscle strength and enhance their physical appearance through sensible strength training. Because the basic strength training principles apply to everyone, I recommend that men and women follow the exercise guidelines presented in Chapter 5.

HOW DO PERSONS OVER 30 RESPOND TO STRENGTH TRAINING?

Persons over 30 respond to strength exercise almost the same as persons under 30. The only difference is the rate of strength gain. During the first two decades of life, your muscles become larger and stronger due to normal growth processes. However, after reaching adulthood, you experience a gradual decrease in your muscle size, physical strength, and metabolic rate.

Fortunately, progressive resistance exercise has a positive effect on these degenerative processes. Regular strength training can maintain your muscle size and strength throughout middle age. Because there is a direct relationship between strong muscles and strong bones, strength exercise may be doubly beneficial for mature men and women.

Another advantage of strength training is increased muscle mass, which results in a higher metabolic rate. As discussed in Chapter 2, additional muscle requires additional calories throughout the day for maintenance and building functions.

Weight training has been accused of causing damage to the heart and circulatory system due to its strenuous nature. Actually, research indicates that sensible strength training may improve cardiovascular function and reduce resting blood pressure. Sensible strength training is characterized by continuous breathing and continuous movement throughout each exercise set. Holding your breath or holding the resistance in a static position for more than a moment may cause a sharp rise in blood pressure and should be avoided. Therefore, whenever you reach a sticking point, you should simply lower the weight. Prolonged straining to complete a final repetition is not necessary for strength development and may present a potential risk for persons over 30 years or those with coronary risk factors.

Because weight training permits a wide range of resistance selections, it is an excellent strength building activity for people of all ages. No matter how weak or strong you are, the resistance may be adjusted so that 10 repetitions can be completed with appropriate effort. This is not always the case for other strength-related exercises, such as calisthenics, in which you are limited to body weight resistance.

If you are over 30, you should follow a sensible program of strength training as presented in Chapter 5. Although you should check with your physician before starting strength training, it has been aptly stated that a medical examination may be more necessary for adults who choose not to exercise.

WHAT ABOUT PROGRESS AND ASSESSMENT?

Although the relationship between strength training and muscle development is reasonably stable over time, it is less predictable on a day-to-day or week-to-week basis. Generally speaking, strength improves at a fast rate during the first few weeks of training. However, as you continue to train, strength gains come more slowly. For example, you may increase your exercise resistance by 20-40 percent during your first month of training but only 2-4 percent during your third month of training.

Basically, the rule of diminishing returns applies to muscle development. At first, simple workouts produce large strength gains. Later, difficult workouts result in small strength gains. This state of affairs, known as a strength plateau, is seldom overcome by doubling or tripling your workout routine. Instead, you should periodically change the training variables to stimulate further strength improvement.

The key to continued progress is gradual improvement and sensitivity to strength plateaus. The strength training logbook is a valuable tool for assessing your progress and for correcting small problems before they become major obstacles. The strength logbook should include the workout date, time, exercises, resistance, repetitions, sets, and notations, such as seat positions and technique adaptations. A sample strength training logbook is presented in the Appendix.

The strength training logbook provides a systematic means for comparing you to yourself, and that is the only meaningful comparison to make. One means for assessing progress is to ask the question, "How does my training today compare with my training four weeks ago?" Continued progress is dependent upon identifying those training procedures that are most effective for producing strength gains. Consequently, people who take a systematic approach to strength training generally achieve better results.

HOW CAN YOU OVERCOME STRENGTH PLATEAUS?

When progress comes to a halt, you are experiencing a strength plateau. This indicates that some aspect of your training program should be altered. The change usually involves one of the following training variables: exercise selection, exercise frequency, exercise sets, repetition–resistance relationship, and exercise intensity.

Although there may be other training considerations (equipment, rest, diet, partners), the basic decision is whether to make your workout more or less demanding. Most exercisers work harder in an attempt to force further strength development. In many cases, this strategy either maintains the plateau or results in strength loss. Doing more of the same activity that led to the strength plateau seldom initiates new strength gains. The better alternative is to examine your training program and make constructive changes that stimulate muscle growth.

Exercise Selection

The first step may be a change in your training exercises. For example, if progress comes to a halt in the bench press, you may substitute the incline press. While both exercises utilize the same muscle groups (chest, shoulders, and triceps), the different movement patterns elicit different muscular responses. Changing your training exercises can stimulate further improvement in both exercise performance and muscle development. As presented in Chapter 9, there are several exercises that may be performed for each of your major muscle groups.

Exercise Frequency

The second consideration has to do with exercise frequency. It is sometimes helpful to reduce your workout demands temporarily to allow the muscle recovery and building processes to catch up. Keep in mind that positive muscle adaptations occur during the rest periods following your training sessions. Consequently, it may be beneficial to schedule more time between successive workouts when facing a strength plateau.

Exercise Sets

A third alternative is to increase or decrease the number of sets per exercise. If you have difficulty training in a high-intensity manner, you may benefit from additional exercise sets. On the other hand, if you are making little progress with multiple-set training, you may achieve better results with a single-set exercise program. As a rule of thumb, the more exercises performed, the fewer sets per exercise.

Repetition-Resistance Relationship

Another area that should be examined is the repetition-resistance relationship. It may be helpful to complete more repetitions at a lower resistance or to perform fewer repetitions at a higher resistance. For example, your quadriceps muscles may be so accustomed to performing 12 repetitions with 140 pounds that this training protocol no longer promotes strength development. If this is the case, switching to eight repetitions with 160 pounds may stimulate the quadriceps to be more responsive. Occasional variations in your repetition-resistance relationship seems to be an effective means for reducing both physical and mental staleness.

Exercise Intensity

You may need to increase your exercise intensity to attain further strength development. Consider the following five techniques for enhancing your training stimulus.

1. Breakdown Training: Breakdown training is an effective means for fatiguing additional muscle fibers immediately following an exercise set. Generally speaking, a set of 10 repetitions fatigues about 25 percent of your muscle fibers. If you immediately reduce the resistance by 10-20 pounds, you can perform a few more repetitions and fatigue a few more muscle fibers. In this manner, you experience muscle failure twice during the extended set of high-effort exercise.

2. Assisted Training: Another high-intensity technique, known as assisted training, accomplishes the same objective with the help of a partner. Instead of reducing the resistance at the point of muscle failure, a partner assists you with a few additional repetitions. To be most effective, your partner provides just enough assistance for you to complete the lifting (positive) movement but allows you to perform the lowering (negative) movement on your own. Three or four assisted repetitions enable you to fatigue more muscle fibers and experience greater strength stimulus during the extended set of high-effort exercise.

3. Negative Training: A third form of high-intensity exercise emphasizes the lowering (negative) movement and is referred to as negative training. Because you can produce about 40 percent more force in a negative contraction than in a positive contraction, you can increase the strength stimulus by emphasizing the lowering movements. Unfortunately, negative training may also increase the risk of injury. It is therefore important to perform negative training in a slow and controlled manner.

As indicated in the previous section, one type of negative training involves a partner who helps you complete a few additional lifting movements but allows you to perform the lowering movements on your own. This procedure emphasizes the negative phase of exercise.

Another type of negative training requires a partner to lift a heavier weight than you can lift on your own. You simply lower the weight load with a slow negative contraction. Due to the inherent risk in this training method, it is important to use just a little more weight than you can lift by yourself.

Negative training may also be helpful for improving your performance in body weight exercises such as pull-ups and bar-dips. If you are not strong enough to lift your body weight, simply climb to the top position and lower yourself very slowly. The same muscles used positively to lift your body are used negatively to lower your body.

4. Super-Slow Training: Another approach to high-intensity exercise is known as super-slow training. Super-slow training is typically characterized by a 10-second lifting movement and a five-second lowering movement. As each repetition requires about 15 seconds, four to six repetitions are sufficient. Because there is almost no momentum, 60-90 seconds of super-slow exercise is very demanding physically and provides an excellent stimulus for strength development.

5. Super-Set Training: Super-set training refers to two successive exercises for the same body part. For example, immediately following a set of triceps extensions, you may perform a set of bar-dips. Both exercises emphasize the triceps muscles but in different movement patterns. Super-set training forces the target muscles to perform double duty. However, because the exact exercise movement is not duplicated, different muscle fibers are involved, and the training stimulus is enhanced.

Strength plateaus appear to be an inevitable consequence of continued training. Regardless of the exercise protocol you follow, there comes a time when change is necessary to stimulate further strength development. The changes you make should be viewed as positive steps toward achieving your full muscular potential.

CAN STRENGTH TRAINING IMPROVE SPEED AND POWER?

Speed and power are often spoken of interchangeably, but they actually represent different physical capacities.

Speed

Speed is an important factor for successful performance in many athletic activities. Most of us would like to increase our movement speed (running speed, throwing speed, striking speed, kicking speed), but this is not an easy task.

Speed is a complex ability that is best improved by repeated practice efforts. Speed training exercises should be performed as quickly as possible to produce the desired results. Because added resistance automatically slows your movement time, strength training may not be very effective for improving your movement speed. For example, a soccer player wants to increase her kicking speed, so she performs fast leg extensions with 30 pounds. Unfortunately, she cannot move a 30-pound weight load nearly as fast as she can kick a soccer ball. Consequently, it is doubtful that this type of strength training will produce a faster kicking action.

Power

Power is the product of movement speed and movement force:

$$Power = Movement\ Speed \times Movement\ Force$$

According to this formula, you may improve your performance power by increasing your movement speed, increasing your movement force, or both. In my opinion, you should perform high-quality skill training to improve your movement speed, and high-intensity strength training to improve your movement force. While your skill training should be specific to your athletic event, your strength training should follow the basic principles presented in Chapter 5. Other things being equal, as you develop greater muscle strength you should experience greater performance power.

Over the past several years, coaches have learned that weight training can increase muscle size and strength without reducing movement speed and joint flexibility. Most athletic coaches therefore include some form of strength training in their sports programs. Participants in team sports (football, soccer, basketball, volleyball, baseball, softball, lacrosse, ice hockey, field hockey), dual sports (tennis, badminton, racquetball, handball, wrestling), and individual sports (track and field, cross-country, swimming and diving, gymnastics, bicycling, canoeing, golf, archery) can all benefit from well-designed strength training programs.

8

Bodybuilding, Strength Building, and Performance Potential

Almost everyone who follows a sensible strength training program experiences a significant degree of muscular development. That is, there is a definite improvement in muscle strength and physical appearance.

While strength exercise produces larger muscle fibers, it does not always produce larger arms or legs. In many cases, the muscle gain is matched by an equal fat loss. However, properly performed strength training does lead to firm, fit, functional muscles that may encourage you to pursue higher levels of development. If you are interested in more muscular size, you may experiment with specific bodybuilding programs. If you are interested in more muscular strength, you may explore specific strength building programs.

Although basic bodybuilding and strength building programs are related, there are differences in the actual training methods. Table 8-1 presents five key training variables associated with typical bodybuilding and strength building programs, as well as guidelines for a combination program.

Table 8-1. Five key training variables associated with typical bodybuilding and strength building programs.

Training variables	Bodybuilding program	Strength building program	Combination program
1. Exercises per muscle group:	3-5 exercises	1-2 exercises	2-3 exercises
2. Sets per exercise:	3-5 sets	4-6 sets	3-4 sets
3. Repetitions per set:	8-12 reps	2-6	5-10 reps
4. Recovery time between sets:	½-1 minute	2½-3 minutes	1½-2 minutes
5. Training days per week:	6 days	3 days	4 days

EXERCISES PER MUSCLE GROUP

Most bodybuilders perform several exercises for each major muscle group. Intermediate bodybuilders typically perform three to five exercises for the thighs, abdominals, chest, upper back, shoulders, biceps, and triceps. In addition, they generally include one or two exercises for the neck, upper trapezius, lower back, oblique, calf, and forearm muscles.

The main reason bodybuilders perform so many exercises is to stimulate more muscle fibers. Because each strength exercise elicits a specific response, a variety of exercises involves more fibers and provides more stimulus for muscle growth.

On the other hand, strength builders are not as concerned about increasing their muscle size. Rather, they strive to achieve high levels of strength performance in specific exercises, such as the squat, deadlift, power clean, bench press, and overhead press. The squat, deadlift, and power clean exercises involve the large muscles of the thigh, buttocks, and lower back. The bench press and overhead press emphasize the muscles of the chest, shoulders, and triceps.

Although most strength builders include additional exercises, they seldom perform more than two exercises per muscle group. This is largely due to time constraints, as strength builders typically complete several sets of each exercise with relatively long recovery periods between sets.

SETS PER EXERCISE

As a rule, both bodybuilders and strength builders perform several sets of each exercise. However, there are notable differences in their training objectives and procedures. The principal reasons bodybuilders do numerous sets are to repetitively stimulate the muscle fibers and to pump up the muscle tissue.

Performing many sets of exercise with brief rests causes large quantities of blood to accumulate in the muscles, increasing their size temporarily. Although not well understood, this temporary muscle enlargement (muscle pump) contributes to the development of larger muscles.

Strength builders perform numerous sets of exercise for other reasons. First, in order to maximize strength, it is necessary to train with heavy resistance. Often strength builders work up to the heaviest weight load they can lift for a single repetition. In order to exercise safely and effectively with such high resistance, they must prepare their muscles for maximum effort by performing progressively heavier warm-up sets. Consequently, the strength builder who ends his workout with a maximum bench press of 300 pounds might perform preliminary sets as follows:

$$140 \text{ pounds} \times 8 \text{ repetitions}$$
$$180 \text{ pounds} \times 6 \text{ repetitions}$$
$$220 \text{ pounds} \times 4 \text{ repetitions}$$
$$260 \text{ pounds} \times 2 \text{ repetitions}$$
$$300 \text{ pounds} \times 1 \text{ repetition}$$

Like bodybuilders, strength builders also perform several sets of exercise to repetitively stimulate the muscle fibers. However, because strength builders are more concerned with muscle performance than muscle pump, they typically rest much longer between sets. For example, a strength builder may perform four sets of leg extensions with 200 pounds and three-minute rests, whereas a bodybuilder may perform four sets of leg extensions with 150 pounds and 30-second rests.

REPETITIONS PER SET

Some individuals have a majority of low endurance muscle fibers and should generally exercise with fewer repetitions per set. Others have a majority of high endurance muscle fibers and should typically train with more repetitions per set. However, there are additional factors that must be considered concerning bodybuilding and strength building.

For bodybuilders to achieve a satisfactory muscle pump, they must perform a reasonably high number of repetitions. Generally speaking, bodybuilders average eight to 12 repetitions per set and occasionally complete as many as 20 repetitions per set.

On the other hand, strength builders exercise with very heavy resistance to facilitate strength gains, thereby necessitating a lower number of repetitions. Although maximum attempts are not uncommon, strength builders usually train with weight loads they can lift for two to six repetitions.

When coupled with short rest periods between sets, eight to 12 repetitions is an effective training range for enhancing muscle size. When coupled with long rest periods between sets, two to six repetitions is a productive training range for increasing muscle strength.

RECOVERY TIME BETWEEN SETS

One of the most critical differences between bodybuilding and strength building is the recovery time between sets of exercise. As mentioned earlier, bodybuilders typically take short rests between sets to maintain blood accumulation within the muscle. This results in temporary muscle enlargement and is referred to as pumping up the muscles. Short-rest strength training is accompanied by considerable muscle discomfort due to blood congestion, lactic acid production, energy depletion, and tissue fatigue. Most bodybuilders rest no more than 30-60 seconds between exercise sets. While this is not the only means for building larger muscles, short rest intervals are characteristic of successful bodybuilding programs.

Strength builders place greater emphasis on muscle performance than muscle appearance and therefore do not intentionally train for a muscle pump. Because exercise resistance is directly related to strength development, strength builders generally train with very heavy weight loads. Of course, this type of training requires relatively long recovery periods for successful performance. This is necessary to establish normal blood flow, remove lactic acid, replenish energy sources, and reduce tissue fatigue. Although the time frame varies among individuals, most strength builders average about three minutes rest between exercise sets.

TRAINING DAYS PER WEEK

Bodybuilders spend a lot of time in the exercise facility. Due to the intense nature of their training program, they generally do not work all of their major muscle groups during a single session. Some bodybuilders follow a two-part split routine, working their legs and lower body on a Monday–Wednesday–Friday sequence and their arms and upper body on a Tuesday–Thursday–Saturday sequence. Others subscribe to a three-part split routine, working their back and biceps on Mondays and Thursdays, their chest and triceps on Tuesdays and Fridays, and their legs and shoulders on Wednesdays and Saturdays.

Although the actual training programs vary considerably, most bodybuilders spend at least six days a week in serious training. It is important to note, however, that they do not intentionally exercise the same muscle group two days in succession.

Conversely, the majority of strength builders take a complete day of rest and recovery between exercise sessions. At the very least, a strength builder may perform all of his exercises on Monday, rest Tuesday, perform all of his exercises again on Wednesday, rest Thursday, etc. However, because heavy training typically requires longer recovery and building periods, an advanced strength builder may emphasize leg exercises on Monday, torso exercises on Wednesday, and a combination of exercises on Friday.

Although specific training schedules vary from individual to individual, it is safe to say that most bodybuilders average six exercise days per week and that the majority of strength builders average three or four exercise days per week.

EVALUATING PERFORMANCE POTENTIAL

While almost everyone can benefit from sensible strength training, some individuals experience better results than others. In fact, there are at least six genetic characteristics that influence your potential for bodybuilding and strength building: (1) frame size, (2) muscle–fat ratio, (3) limb length, (4) tendon attachments, (5) muscle length, and (6) muscle fiber type. Each of these factors should be considered when setting performance goals and evaluating training progress.

Frame Size

You have inherited a particular frame size that includes your height, width, and depth as viewed from the front. You may be tall or short, have a wide shoulder girdle or a narrow shoulder girdle, and have a large rib cage structure or a small rib cage structure. These are all genetic characteristics over which you have little control.

Generally speaking, both bodybuilders and strength builders benefit from above-average frame size. While height is not usually a limitation, a large bone structure (wide shoulder girdle, deep rib cage) is definitely advantageous for developing muscle size and strength.

Sometimes frame size is referred to as your somatotype, which generally falls into one of three categories: (1) *endomorphic* individuals are characterized by a round, overweight appearance; (2) *ectomorphic* individuals exhibit a linear, underweight appearance; and (3) *mesomorphic* individuals have rectangular, muscular physiques and are most successful in bodybuilding and strength building endeavors.

Muscle-Fat Ratio

Your somatotype is also related to your muscle–fat ratio. Endomorphs are typically above-average in fat and below-average in muscle, resulting in a soft appearance. Ectomorphs generally have below-average fat and below-average muscle, resulting in a slender appearance. Mesomorphs usually have below-average fat and above-average muscle, resulting in a strong appearance.

Like frame size, your muscle–fat ratio is largely determined through genetics. You have a specific number of muscle fibers. Strength training causes an increase in the size but not the number of your muscle fibers, resulting in larger and stronger muscles (hypertrophy). Conversely, lack of strength training causes a decrease in the size but not the number of your muscle fibers, leading to smaller and weaker muscles (atrophy).

In a similar manner, you have a specific number of fat cells, the purpose of which is to store energy reserves in the form of fat. Eating more calories than you need for your daily energy requirements causes an increase in the size but not the number of your fat cells, resulting in a softer appearance. Eating fewer calories than you need for your daily energy requirements causes a decrease in the size but not the number of your fat cells, resulting in a harder appearance.

It is possible for you to increase the size of your muscle fibers and to decrease the size of your fat cells. However, persons who have inherited a large number of muscle fibers and a small number of fat cells certainly have an advantage in this regard.

Limb Length

Limb length is probably not of major concern to bodybuilders, as other factors have much greater influence on muscle size. However, limb length may affect your ability to demonstrate muscle strength.

For example, persons with long arms seldom have great success in the bench press. Consider that the amount of work performed equals the resistance times the distance it is lifted. Consequently, individuals with long arms must push the barbell a greater distance and perform more work than persons with short arms. The same disadvantage holds true for long-legged individuals performing squats or deadlifts.

This is not to imply that persons with long limbs should avoid strength building exercises but only that it may be more difficult for them to demonstrate strength.

Tendon Attachments

The point of tendon attachment is very important to strength performance. As discussed in Chapter 4, the point where your muscle tendon inserts at the bone provides a distinct leverage advantage or disadvantage.

Recall the example in which two women each have 10-inch forearms and can produce exactly 200 pounds of force in their biceps muscles. If both women have biceps tendon insertion points that are one inch from the elbow joint, they both will be capable of holding a 20-pound dumbbell at a right angle.

Muscle Force × Force Arm = Resistance × Resistance Arm
200 pounds × 1 inch = 20 pounds × 10 inches

However, if one woman's biceps tendon insertion point is only three-quarters inch from her elbow joint, she will be capable of holding only a 15-pound dumbbell at a right angle.

Muscle Force × Force Arm = Resistance × Resistance Arm
200 pounds × ¾ inch = 15 pounds × 10 inches

Even though limb length and muscle force capacity are identical, a minor difference in the point of tendon insertion can make a major difference in strength performance. The further the tendon inserts from the joint axis, the greater the leverage advantage and the greater the functional strength.

Sometimes it is possible to observe favorable tendon attachments, and sometimes it is not. Generally speaking, persons who produce more strength than seems indicated by their outward appearance have favorable tendon attachments.

Muscle Length

As discussed in Chapter 4, muscle length refers to the distance between the two tendon attachments. Other things being equal, relatively long muscles have greater potential for developing size and strength.

Estimating Your Muscle Length: A method for assessing your muscle length involves careful observation of some prominent muscles. Although muscle length may vary somewhat from muscle to muscle, I recommend checking at least the following two muscle groups.

1. Calves: Standing in front of a floor-length mirror, rise onto your toes and carefully observe the lower end of your calf muscle. If the bulge stops about midway between your knee and ankle, you have medium length calf muscles. If the bulge disappears about one-third the distance from your knee to your ankle, you have short calf muscles. If the bulge continues two-thirds the distance from your knee to your ankle, you have long calf muscles (see Figure 8-1).

2. Biceps: With your elbow at a right angle and your fist turned inward, see

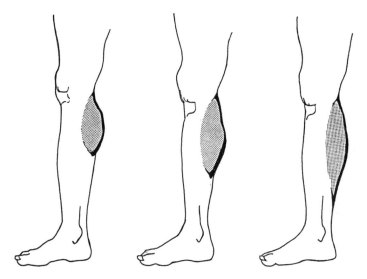

Figure 8-1. Comparison of short, medium, and long calf muscles.

how many fingers you can comfortably place between your forearm and the end of your contracted biceps muscle. If you can insert two fingers, you have medium length biceps muscles. If you can insert three fingers, you have short biceps muscles. If you can insert only one finger, you have long biceps muscles (see Figure 8-2).

Muscle Fiber Type

As discussed in Chapter 4, fast-twitch muscle fibers are relatively large and have high growth potential. Conversely, slow-twitch muscle fibers are relatively small and have low growth potential. Other things being equal, muscles with predominantly fast-twitch fibers have greater potential for developing size and strength.

Estimating Your Muscle Fiber Type: One means for estimating your muscle fiber type is determining the number of repetitions you can complete with 75 percent of your maximum resistance. Because muscle fiber type may vary somewhat from muscle to muscle, I suggest testing at least one muscle group from the lower body and one muscle group from the upper body. As an example, consider the following assessment procedure for the front thigh (quadriceps) muscles using a leg extension machine.

1. Perform 10 warm-up repetitions with a light weight load (30 percent of body weight).
2. Rest two minutes.

Figure 8-2. Comparison of short, medium, and long biceps muscles.

3. Perform five repetitions with a medium weight load (50 percent of body weight).
4. Rest two minutes.
5. Perform one repetition with a heavy weight load (70 percent of body weight).
6. Rest two minutes.
7. Continue in this manner until you find the maximum weight load that you can lift one time.
8. Rest five minutes.
9. Perform as many repetitions as possible with 75 percent of your maximum weight load.

If you complete from eight to 13 repetitions with 75 percent of your maximum resistance, you most likely have an even mix of fibers (about 50 percent fast-twitch and 50 percent slow-twitch) in this muscle group. If you complete less than eight repetitions, you probably have a majority of fast-twitch fibers in this muscle group. If you complete more than 13 repetitions, you probably have a majority of slow-twitch fibers in this muscle group.

Table 8-2 summarizes the key physical characteristics associated with successful bodybuilders and strength builders. With the possible exceptions of limb length and tendon attachments, successful bodybuilders and strength builders share similar genetic advantages. Generally speaking, both bodybuilders and strength builders benefit from large frame size, high muscle-to-fat ratios, long muscle bellies, and predominantly fast-twitch muscle fibers. Consequently, the differences in their physical development (large muscle size versus high muscle strength) is mostly due to their specific training methods.

Table 8-2. Comparison of key physical characteristics associated with successful bodybuilders and strength builders.

Physical characteristics	Successful bodybuilders	Successful strength builders
Frame size	Large	Large
Muscle–Fat ratio	High muscle–Low fat (Mesomorph)	High muscle–Low fat (Mesomorph)
Limb length	Varies	Relatively short
Tendon attachments	Varies	Favorable insertion points
Muscle length	Long muscle bellies	Long muscle bellies
Muscle fiber type	Predominantly fast-twitch	Predominantly fast-twitch

DESIGNING A TRAINING PROGRAM

The muscle groups that bodybuilders should train to attain a well-developed and well-balanced physique are listed in Table 8-3. This table lists major and minor muscle groups of the body and presents sample strength exercises for each. It is noted that bodybuilders usually approach their training in terms of muscle groups rather than selected strength exercises.

Table 8-3. Major and minor muscle groups and suggested exercises for bodybuilders.

Major muscle groups	Suggested exercises
Quadriceps	Squat, leg press, leg extension, deadlift
Hamstrings	Squat, leg press, leg curl, deadlift
Hip adductors	Adductor machine
Hip abductors	Abductor machine
Lower back	Low-back machine, deadlift
Abdominals	Abdominal machine, weighted trunk curl
Obliques	Rotary torso machine, twist trunk curl
Chest	Bench press, incline press, bar-dip, cross chest machine, 10-degree chest machine, chest fly
Upper back	Pulldown, seated row, dumbbell bent row, pullover machine, chin-up
Shoulders	Standing press, upright row, lateral raise machine, neck and shoulder machine, shrug
Biceps	Standing curl, incline dumbbell curl, biceps machine, preacher curl, chin-up
Triceps	Pressdown, bar-dip, standing extension, lying extension, triceps machine, kickback
Neck flexors	Neck machine, manual resistance
Neck extensors	Neck machine, manual resistance
Minor muscle groups	
Wrist flexors	Standing curl, wrist roller
Wrist extensors	Wrist roller
Calves	Standing heel raise
Shins	Seated toe raise

Strength builders, especially competitive weightlifters, typically take the opposite approach. That is, they generally focus on a few basic exercises with one or two supplementary ones added for enhancing their overall muscle strength. Table 8-4 presents the basic and supplementary exercises along with the prime mover muscle groups used in each lift.

Although no two bodybuilders or strength builders should follow identical exercise programs, it is often helpful to examine representative training protocols. Table 8-5 presents a sample weekly exercise program for intermediate bodybuilders, and Table 8-6 presents a sample program for intermediate strength builders. While it is not recommended that you follow these exercise protocols precisely, they do serve as guidelines for more specialized programs in bodybuilding or strength building.

Individuals who do not desire to become competitive bodybuilders or strength builders but would like to achieve both additional muscle size and strength may experiment with a combination program. As presented in Table 8-1, a combination program attempts to balance the training variables with a moderate number of exercises, sets, repetitions, training days, and recovery time.

Table 8-4. Basic and supplementary exercises for strength builders.

Basic exercises	Prime mover muscle groups
Barbell squat	Quadriceps, hamstrings, gluteals, lower back
Deadlift	Quadriceps, hamstrings, gluteals, lower back
Power clean	Quadriceps, hamstrings, gluteals, lower back, upper back, shoulders, trapezius, biceps, calves
Bench press	Chest, shoulders, triceps
Standing press	Shoulders, trapezius, triceps
Supplementary exercises	
Leg extension	Quadriceps
Leg curl	Hamstrings
Low-back machine	Lower back
Abdominal machine	Abdominals
Rotary torso machine	Obliques
Chest cross machine	Chest
Incline press	Chest
Bar-dip	Triceps, chest
Seated row	Upper back
Pulldown	Upper back
Lateral raise machine	Shoulders
Standing curl	Biceps
Pressdown	Triceps
Wrist roll	Wrist flexors, wrist extensors
Heel raise	Calves
Toe raise	Shins
Shrug	Trapezius

Table 8-5. Sample training program for intermediate bodybuilders.

Monday (back, biceps, abdominals)
  Back exercises
Deadlift	3 sets (12-10-8)	60 sec. rest
Pulldown	3 sets (12-10-8)	60 sec. rest
Seated row	3 sets (12-10-8)	60 sec. rest
Pullover machine	3 sets (12-10-8)	60 sec. rest
Chin-up	3 sets (10-8-6)	45 sec. rest

  Biceps exercises
Standing curl	4 sets (12-10-8-6)	45 sec. rest
Incline dumbbell curl	4 sets (12-10-8-6)	45 sec. rest
Preacher curl	4 sets (12-10-8-6)	45 sec. rest
Biceps machine	4 sets (12-10-8-6)	30 sec. rest

  Abdominal exercises
Abdominal machine	3 sets (12-10-8)	30 sec. rest
Trunk curl/weight	3 sets (20-15-10)	30 sec. rest
Rotary torso machine	2 sets (12/12-10/10)	30 sec. rest

Tuesday (chest, triceps, neck, forearms)
  Chest exercises
Bench press	4 sets (12-10-8-6)	60 sec. rest
Incline press	3 sets (12-10-8)	60 sec. rest
Cross chest machine	3 sets (12-10-8)	60 sec. rest
10-degree chest machine	3 sets (12-10-8)	60 sec. rest
Bar-dip	3 sets (10-8-6)	45 sec. rest

  Triceps exercises
Pressdown	4 sets (12-10-8-6)	45 sec. rest
Lying extension	4 sets (12-10-8-6)	45 sec. rest
Triceps machine	4 sets (12-10-8-6)	45 sec. rest
Standing extension	4 sets (12-10-8-6)	30 sec. rest

  Neck exercises
Neck flexor machine	3 sets (12-10-8)	45 sec. rest
Neck extensor machine	3 sets (12-10-8)	45 sec. rest

  Forearm exercises
Wrist roll	2 sets (8/8-6/6)	60 sec. rest

Wednesday (legs, shoulders, calves)
  Leg exercises
Squat	4 sets (12-10-8-6)	60 sec. rest
Leg extension machine	4 sets (12-10-8-6)	60 sec. rest
Leg curl machine	4 sets (12-10-8-6)	60 sec. rest
Leg press machine	4 sets (12-10-8-6)	60 sec. rest
Hip adductor machine	3 sets (12-10-8)	60 sec. rest
Hip abductor machine	3 sets (12-10-8)	60 sec. rest

  Shoulder exercises
Standing press	4 sets (12-10-8-6)	60 sec. rest
Upright row	4 sets (12-10-8-6)	45 sec. rest
Lateral raise machine	4 sets (12-10-8-6)	45 sec. rest
Neck & shoulder machine	3 sets (12-10-8)	30 sec. rest

  Calf exercises
Standing heel raise	3 sets (12-10-8)	30 sec. rest
Seated heel raise	3 sets (12-10-8)	30 sec. rest

Thursday — same as Monday   *Friday — same as Tuesday*

Saturday — same as Wednesday   *Sunday — rest*

Table 8-6. Sample training program for intermediate strength builders.

Monday		
Barbell squat	6 sets progressive (8-6-4-2-2-2)	3 min. rest
Leg extension	4 sets (6-6-6-6)	3 min. rest
Leg curl	4 sets (6-6-6-6)	3 min. rest
Pulldown	4 sets (6-6-6-6)	3 min. rest
Seated row	4 sets (6-6-6-6)	3 min. rest
Standing curl	4 sets (6-6-6-6)	3 min. rest
Heel raise	4 sets (8-8-8-8)	2 min. rest
Wednesday		
Bench press	6 sets progressive (8-6-4-3-3-3)	3 min. rest
Standing press	4 sets (6-6-6-6)	3 min. rest
Bar-dip	4 sets (6-6-6-6)	3 min. rest
Pressdown	4 sets (6-6-6-6)	3 min. rest
Lateral raise machine	4 sets (8-8-8-8)	3 min. rest
Shrug	4 sets (4-4-4-4)	2 min. rest
Friday		
Deadlift	6 sets progressive (8-6-4-2-2-2)	3 min. rest
Power clean	6 sets (8-6-4-2-2-2)	3 min. rest
Abdominal machine	4 sets (8-8-8-8)	3 min. rest
Low-back machine	4 sets (6-6-6-6)	3 min. rest
Rotary torso machine	2 sets (6/6-6/6)	3 min. rest
Wrist roll	2 sets (6/6-6/6)	2 min. rest

Tuesday, Thursday, Saturday, and Sunday are non-strength training days.

BASIC VERSUS SPECIALIZED TRAINING

The basic recommendations for sensible strength exercise presented in the preceding chapters work well. Most men and women who follow these guidelines for safe, effective, and efficient strength exercise will be highly satisfied with the results.

However, if you have both the genetic potential and personal motivation to become a bodybuilder or strength builder, the information presented in this chapter provides a basis for more specialized training. These training programs require a lot of time and effort. Examine your personal objectives, evaluate your physical potential, and consider your training commitment. If "all systems are go," review the sample programs and tailor the training variables to your own exercise circumstances. With a systematic approach and attention to body feedback, you should make good progress towards your training goals.

9
Strength Training Exercises

Strength training exercises should be selected on the basis of safety and effectiveness. In terms of safety, each exercise should have a low risk of injury when performed properly. In terms of effectiveness, each exercise should provide a strength stimulus to the target muscle groups.

The 60 exercises illustrated in this chapter meet these standards. The first section describes exercises for each of the major muscle groups using free-weight equipment (barbells and dumbbells). The second section presents similar exercises performed on single-station weight-stack machines. The third section highlights basic exercises utilizing single-station barbell plate machines. The fourth section discusses exercises done on multi-station weight-stack machines.

Exercises that involve one muscle group produce curved movements and are referred to as rotary exercises. Exercises that involve two or more muscle groups produce straight movements and are referred to as linear exercises.

The exercises are presented from larger muscle groups to smaller muscle groups and should be executed in this order whenever possible. Each exercise should be performed slowly through a full range of movement.

PROPER BREATHING TECHNIQUE

Before you start the strength training exercises, it is important to understand proper breathing technique. Be sure to breathe continuously during each set of exercise. Never hold your breath, as this can cause a sharp rise in blood pressure.

The best breathing pattern is to exhale during each lifting movement and to inhale during each lowering movement. This maintains a favorable balance between your external muscle pressure and your internal air pressure.

FREE WEIGHTS: BARBELLS AND DUMBBELLS

Figure 9-1. Barbell squat.

Barbell Squat

The barbell squat (see Figure 9-1) is a linear exercise that involves the quadriceps, hamstrings, and gluteal muscles.

Technical Points:

1. Stand with feet shoulder width apart.
2. Place barbell across upper back and secure with a wide handgrip.
3. Carefully lift barbell from standards and hold momentarily in standing position.
4. Keeping the back erect and head up, slowly lower the hips until the thighs are parallel to the floor.
5. Keeping the back erect and head up, slowly extend upward to the standing position.
6. Carefully return barbell to standards after last repetition.

Note: It is important to maintain an erect back and head-up posture throughout the exercise. It is not advisable to drop below a thigh-parallel-to-the-floor position. Be sure to use a spotter on this exercise.

Figure 9-2. Dumbbell lunge.

Dumbbell Lunge

The dumbbell lunge (see Figure 9-2) is a linear exercise that includes the quadriceps, hamstrings, and gluteal muscles.

Technical Points:

1. Stand erect with a dumbbell in each hand.
2. Step forward with the right foot into a straddle position.
3. Step backward with the right foot to the original standing position.
4. Step forward with the left foot into a straddle position.
5. Step backward with the left foot to the original standing position.

Note: Maintain an erect torso posture throughout the exercise. The exercise difficulty may be increased by taking larger steps. Try to keep your forward knee directly over your foot as you step into the straddle position.

Figure 9-3. Barbell deadlift.

Barbell Deadlift

The barbell deadlift (see Figure 9-3) is a linear exercise that involves the quadriceps, hamstrings, gluteal, low-back, and shoulder muscles.

Technical Points:

1. Squat above barbell with feet shoulder width apart, back straight, and head up.
2. Grasp barbell with a mixed (one overhand, one underhand) grip.
3. Keeping the arms straight, bring the barbell to the upper thighs by slowly extending the knees and hips.
4. Pause briefly in the standing position and slowly return barbell to the floor.

Note: Keep the back straight and head up throughout the exercise. The arms remain straight, as the lifting force is produced by the powerful muscles of the thighs and hips.

Figure 9-4. Barbell bench press.

Barbell Bench Press

The barbell bench press (see Figure 9-4) is a linear exercise that utilizes the chest, front shoulder, and triceps muscles.

Technical Points:

1. Lie on bench with feet on floor.
2. Place hands evenly on barbell, slightly wider than shoulders.
3. Lift barbell from standards.
4. Slowly lower barbell to midchest, touching lightly.
5. Slowly push barbell upward to near lockout position.
6. Carefully return barbell to standards after last repetition.

Note: The head, shoulders, and hips should remain on the bench throughout the exercise. The actual barbell path is from midchest in the bottom position to above the neck in the top position. Be sure to use a spotter on this exercise.

Figure 9-5. Barbell incline press.

Barbell Incline Press

The barbell incline press (see Figure 9-5) is a linear exercise that addresses the upper chest, front shoulder, and triceps muscles.

Technical Points:

1. Sit on bench with feet on floor.
2. Place hands evenly on barbell, wider than shoulders.
3. Lift barbell from standards.
4. Slowly lower barbell to upper chest, touching lightly.
5. Slowly push barbell upward to near lockout position.
6. Carefully return barbell to standards after last repetition.

Note: The head and shoulders should remain on the bench throughout the exercise. Be sure to use a spotter on this exercise.

Figure 9-6. Dumbbell chest fly.

Dumbbell Chest Fly

The dumbbell chest fly (see Figure 9-6) is a rotary exercise that targets the chest and front shoulder muscles.

Technical Points:

1. Lie on bench with feet on floor, footrest, or stool.
2. Hold dumbbells above chest with arms extended.
3. Slowly lower dumbbells downward and outward until they are at chest level, with the elbows slightly bent.
4. Slowly lift dumbbells upward and inward to the starting position.

Note: The head, shoulders, and hips should remain on the bench throughout the exercise. The elbows should be flexed during the lifting and lowering movements. Due to leverage factors, dumbbell chest flies should be performed in a slow and controlled manner.

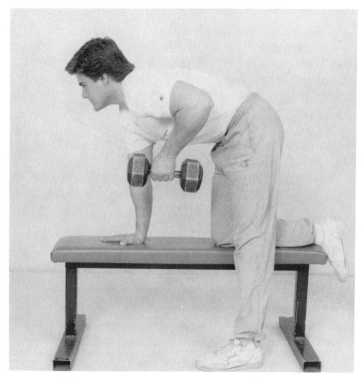

Figure 9-7. Dumbbell bent row.

Dumbbell Bent Row

The dumbbell bent row (see Figure 9-7) is a linear exercise that involves the upper back and biceps muscles.

Technical Points:

1. Bend at waist and place one hand on bench so that back is parallel to floor.
2. Hold dumbbell at arm's length with free hand.
3. Slowly pull dumbbell to chest and pause momentarily.
4. Slowly lower dumbbell to starting position and repeat.
5. Repeat the above procedures with the other arm.

Note: Keep one hand on the bench at all times for back support.

Figure 9-8. Weighted pull-up.

Weighted Pull-Up

The weighted pull-up (see Figure 9-8) is a linear exercise that includes the upper back, rear shoulder, and biceps muscles.

Technical Points:

1. Grasp the bar with an underhand, shoulder-width grip.
2. From a full hang position, slowly lift body until chin is above the bar and hold momentarily.
3. Slowly lower body to full hang position and repeat.

Note: This exercise should be performed with a relatively straight body and neutral head position. Weight plates are typically attached by means of a rope around the waist.

Figure 9-9. Barbell press.

Barbell Press

The barbell press (see Figure 9-9) is a linear exercise that involves the shoulder, trapezius, and triceps muscles.

Technical Points:

1. Stand in front of barbell standards with feet shoulder width apart.
2. Using an overhand, shoulder-width grip, lift barbell from the standards and hold at shoulder level.
3. Slowly push barbell upward to near lockout position.
4. Slowly lower barbell to shoulder level and repeat.
5. Return barbell to standards after final repetition.

Note: Maintain a relatively straight back and neutral head position throughout the exercise. Arching backward may place excessive stress on the lower back.

Figure 9-10. Alternate dumbbell press.

Alternate Dumbbell Press

The alternate dumbbell press (see Figure 9-10) is a linear movement that addresses the shoulder, trapezius, and triceps muscles.

Technical Points:

1. Begin with feet shoulder width apart and dumbbells at shoulder level.
2. Slowly press right arm upward to near lockout position and lower to shoulder level.
3. Slowly press left arm upward to near lockout position and lower to shoulder level.
4. Continue to alternate right arm presses and left arm presses.

Note: Maintain a relatively straight back and neutral head position throughout the exercise. Performing overhead presses one arm at a time places less stress on the lower back.

Figure 9-11. Barbell upright row.

Barbell Upright Row

The barbell upright row (see Figure 9-11) is a linear exercise that involves the shoulder, trapezius, and biceps muscles.

Technical Points:

1. Stand with feet shoulder width apart.
2. Hold barbell at waist level with very narrow hand spacing.
3. Leading with the elbows, slowly pull barbell straight up to chin and pause momentarily.
4. Slowly lower barbell to starting position.

Note: Torso should be erect and head in neutral position throughout the exercise. Be sure to lead each lifting movement with the elbows.

Figure 9-12. Dumbbell lateral raise.

Dumbbell Lateral Raise

The dumbbell lateral raise (see Figure 9-12) is a rotary exercise that largely isolates the shoulder muscles.

Technical Points:

1. Stand with feet shoulder width apart and hold dumbbells at sides.
2. Leading with bent elbows, slowly lift arms upward and sideward until dumbbells are at shoulder level.
3. After a momentary pause, slowly lower arms to starting position.

Note: Maintain an erect posture and neutral head position throughout the exercise. Be sure to lead each lifting movement with bent elbows.

Figure 9-13. Dumbbell bent lateral raise.

Dumbbell Bent Lateral Raise

The dumbbell bent lateral raise (see Figure 9-13) is a rotary exercise that emphasizes the rear shoulder muscles.

Technical Points:

1. Stand with feet shoulder width apart, bend forward slightly at the hips, and hold dumbbells in hanging position.
2. Leading with bent elbows, slowly lift arms upward and sideward until dumbbells are at shoulder level.
3. After a momentary pause, slowly lower arms to starting position.

Note: Be sure to lead each lifting movement with bent elbows.

Figure 9-14. Dumbbell front lateral raise.

Dumbbell Front Lateral Raise

The dumbbell front lateral raise (see Figure 9-14) is a rotary exercise that emphasizes the front shoulder muscles.

Technical Points:

1. Stand with feet shoulder width apart and hold dumbbells at sides.
2. Leading with bent elbows, slowly lift arms upward and frontward until dumbbells are at shoulder level.
3. After a momentary pause, slowly lower arms to starting position.

Note: Maintain an erect posture and neutral head position throughout the exercise. Be sure to lead each lifting movement with bent elbows.

Figure 9-15. Barbell curl.

Barbell Curl

The barbell curl (see Figure 9-15) is a rotary exercise for the biceps muscles.

Technical Points:

1. Stand with feet shoulder width apart and hold barbell at thigh level, palms up.
2. Keeping elbows at sides, slowly lift barbell to shoulder level.
3. After a momentary pause, slowly lower barbell to starting position.

Note: Maintain a straight back and neutral head position throughout the exercise. Be sure to keep elbows at sides during each lifting and lowering movement. A cambered barbell may be preferred for this exercise.

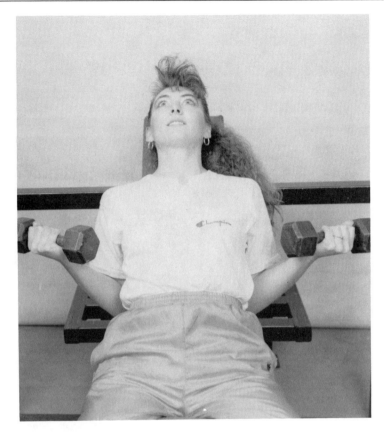

Figure 9-16. Incline dumbbell curl.

Incline Dumbbell Curl

The incline dumbbell curl (see Figure 9-16) is a rotary exercise that largely isolates the biceps muscles.

Technical Points:

1. Sit on seat and hold dumbbells at sides, palms up.
2. Slowly lift dumbbells to shoulder level and pause momentarily.
3. Slowly return dumbbells to starting position and repeat.

Note: Keep back firmly pressed against seat back throughout the exercise. Elbows should remain in approximately the same position during each lifting and lowering movement. Thumbs should be turned away from the body for maximum biceps involvement.

Figure 9-17. Preacher dumbbell curl.

Preacher Dumbbell Curl

The preacher dumbbell curl (see Figure 9-17) is a rotary exercise that addresses the biceps muscles.

Technical Points:

1. Sit on preacher bench with elbows securely positioned on support pad.
2. Hold dumbbells in arm extended position, palms up.
3. Slowly lift dumbbells until biceps are fully contracted and pause momentarily.
4. Slowly lower dumbbells to starting position.

Note: Torso should be erect and head in neutral position throughout the exercise. Thumbs should be turned away from the body for maximum biceps involvement.

Figure 9-18. Standing dumbbell triceps extension.

Standing Dumbbell Triceps Extension

The standing dumbbell triceps extension (see Figure 9-18) is a rotary exercise that targets the triceps muscles.

Technical Points:

1. Stand with feet shoulder width apart.
2. Hold dumbbell in both hands, with arms nearly extended overhead.
3. Without changing elbow position, slowly lower dumbbell behind neck.
4. After momentary pause, slowly lift dumbbell to starting position.

Note: Torso should remain erect throughout the exercise. Head may be held slightly downward if desired. Be sure to keep the elbows high during the lowering and lifting movements.

Figure 9-19. Lying barbell triceps extension.

Lying Barbell Triceps Extension

The lying barbell triceps extension (see Figure 9-19) is a rotary exercise that emphasizes the triceps muscles.

Technical Points:

1. Lie on bench and grasp barbell with close, overhand grip.
2. Begin with arms nearly extended above chest.
3. Keeping elbows high, slowly lower barbell to forehead and pause momentarily.
4. Keeping elbows high, slowly lift barbell to starting position.

Note: Elbows should remain in approximately the same position during the lowering and lifting movements. A cambered barbell may be preferred for this exercise.

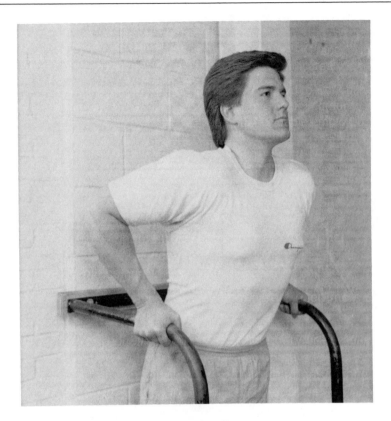

Figure 9-20. Weighted bar-dip.

Weighted Bar-Dip

The weighted bar-dip (see Figure 9-20) is a linear exercise that includes the chest, front shoulder, and triceps muscles.

Technical Points:

1. Begin in a supported position with arms nearly extended.
2. Slowly lower body until upper arms are parallel to floor.
3. Slowly lift body to starting position.

Note: This exercise should be performed with a relatively straight body and neutral head position. Weight plates are typically attached by means of a rope around the waist.

Figure 9-21. Barbell shoulder shrug.

Barbell Shoulder Shrug

The barbell shoulder shrug (see Figure 9-21) is a rotary exercise for the trapezius (upper back and neck) muscles.

Technical Points:

1. Stand with feet shoulder width apart and hold barbell at thigh level, palms down.
2. Keeping the arms straight, lift barbell a few inches by slowly elevating the shoulders in a shrugging movement.
3. After a momentary pause, slowly lower barbell to starting position.

Note: Keep the back straight and head in a neutral position throughout the exercise. The arms remain straight, as the lifting force is produced by the trapezius muscles.

Figure 9-22. Barbell heel raise.

Barbell Heel Raise

The barbell heel raise (see Figure 9-22) is a rotary exercise that largely isolates the calf muscles.

Technical Points:

1. Stand with toes on platform and feet shoulder width apart.
2. Place barbell across upper back and secure with wide handgrip.
3. Carefully lift barbell from standards and hold in a standing position.
4. Keeping back erect and head in neutral position, slowly raise heels as high as possible and pause momentarily.
5. Slowly lower heels until the calf muscles are comfortably stretched and repeat.

Note: Due to the short movement range, this exercise should be performed very slowly. Generally, this exercise requires a relatively heavy resistance.

Figure 9-23. Toe raise.

Toe Raise

The toe raise (see Figure 9-23) is a rotary exercise that targets the shin muscles.

Technical Points:

1. Sit on high seat with knee at right angle.
2. Attach weight plate to foot with thin rope.
3. Slowly raise toes towards shins as far as possible and pause momentarily.
4. Slowly lower toes as far as possible and repeat.
5. Repeat the above procedures with the other foot.

Note: Due to the short movement range, this exercise should be performed very slowly. Generally, this exercise requires a relatively light resistance.

Figure 9-24. Wrist roll.

Wrist Roll

The wrist roll (see Figure 9-24) is a rotary exercise that involves the forearm flexor and forearm extensor muscles.

Technical Points:

1. Stand with feet shoulder width apart, and hold bar away from body in an overhand grip.
2. Turning the hands clockwise in an alternate manner, slowly roll the weighted rope onto the bar as far as possible. This movement uses the forearm flexor muscles.
3. Turning the hands counterclockwise in an alternate manner, slowly roll the weighted rope off the bar until it is completely unwound. This movement uses the forearm extensor muscles.

Note: Cover as much distance as possible with each wrist movement. Generally, this exercise requires a relatively light resistance.

Figure 9-25. Weighted trunk curl.

Weighted Trunk Curl

The weighted trunk curl (see Figure 9-25) is a rotary exercise that addresses the abdominal muscles.

Technical Points:

1. Lie on floor with knees bent, and hold weight plate behind head or on upper chest.
2. Slowly lift head and shoulders off floor while pressing lower back into floor.
3. After a momentary pause, slowly lower head and shoulders to floor and repeat.

Note: Maintain the head in a neutral position as much as possible. Due to the short movement range, this exercise should be performed very slowly. Generally, this exercise requires a relatively light resistance.

SINGLE-STATION WEIGHT-STACK MACHINES

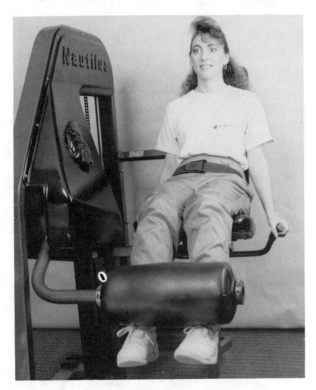

Figure 9-26. Leg extension.

Leg Extension Machine

The leg extension (see Figure 9-26) is a rotary exercise that largely isolates the quadriceps muscles.

Technical Points:

1. Sit on seat and align knee joints with machine axis of rotation.
2. Use additional pad for back support if necessary.
3. Fasten seat belt.
4. Place hands on handgrips.
5. Place ankles in neutral position behind roller pad.
6. Slowly lift roller pad until the quadriceps are fully contracted and hold momentarily.
7. Slowly lower roller pad until plates almost touch weight stack and repeat.

Note: By not allowing the plates to rest on the weight stack, muscle tension is maintained throughout the exercise set. The lower back should remain in contact with the seat back throughout this exercise.

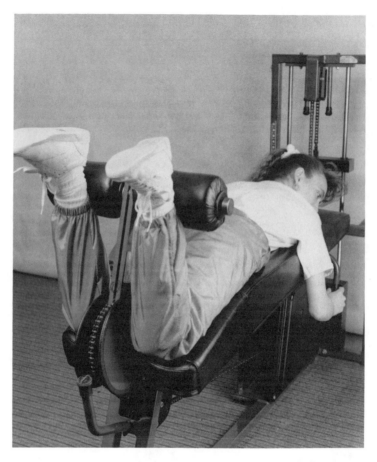

Figure 9-27. Leg curl.

Leg Curl Machine

The leg curl (see Figure 9-27) is a rotary exercise that largely isolates the hamstring muscles.

Technical Points:

1. Lie on seat and align knee joints with machine axis of rotation.
2. Place hands on handgrips.
3. Place ankles in neutral position behind roller pads.
4. Slowly lift roller pads until the hamstrings are fully contracted and hold momentarily.
5. Slowly lower roller pads until plates almost touch weight stack and repeat.

Note: For complete contraction of the hamstring muscles, the hips must raise slightly off the support pad but should be supported as much as possible.

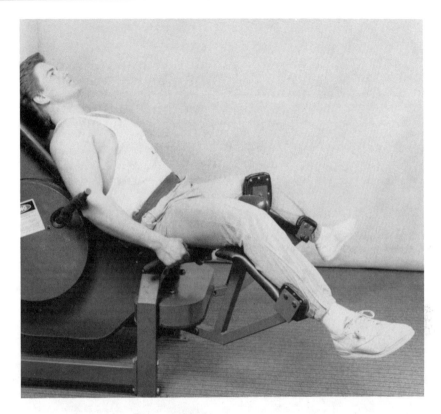

Figure 9-28. Hip adduction.

Hip Adduction Machine

The hip adduction (see Figure 9-28) is a rotary exercise that targets the inner thigh muscles.

Technical Points:

1. Sit on seat with back fully supported.
2. Fasten seat belt.
3. Place hands on handgrips.
4. Place legs outside knee pads.
5. Slowly move legs together and hold momentarily in final position.
6. Slowly move legs apart until comfortably stretched and repeat.

Note: Assistance may be necessary to place the legs into the starting position.

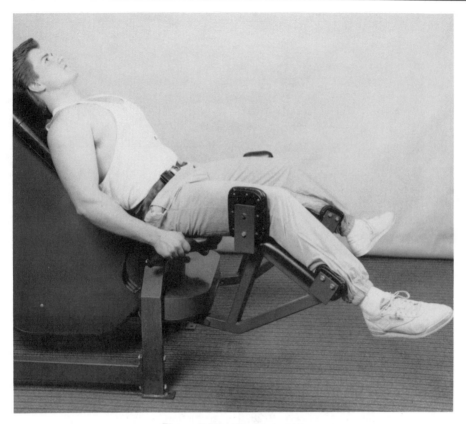

Figure 9-29. Hip abduction.

Hip Abduction Machine

The hip abduction (see Figure 9-29) is a rotary exercise that largely isolates the outer thigh muscles.

Technical Points:

1. Sit on seat with back fully supported.
2. Fasten seat belt.
3. Place hands on handgrips.
4. Place legs inside knee pads.
5. Slowly move legs apart and hold momentarily in final position.
6. Slowly move legs together until plates almost touch weight stack and repeat.

Note: It is important to attain a full range of movement in this exercise.

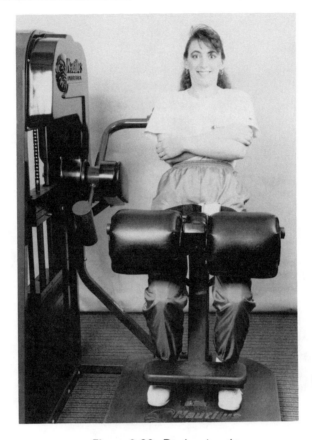

Figure 9-30. Back extension.

Low-Back Machine

The back extension (see Figure 9-30) is a rotary exercise that emphasizes the low-back muscles.

Technical Points:

1. Sit on seat in front of roller pad with feet evenly spaced on floor grid.
2. Fasten thigh belt and secure thigh pads.
3. Fold arms across chest and keep head in neutral position.
4. Slowly push roller pad backward to extended position and pause momentarily.
5. Return slowly until plates almost touch weight stack and repeat.

Note: It is important to perform all lower back movements slowly.

Figure 9-31. Abdominal curl.

Abdominal Machine

The abdominal curl (see Figure 9-31) is a rotary exercise that emphasizes the abdominal muscles.

Technical Points:

1. Sit on seat behind torso pads, with feet secured beneath foot rollers.
2. Place hands across abdomen or behind back.
3. Slowly push torso pads forward about 30 degrees and pause momentarily.
4. Return slowly until plates almost touch weight stack and repeat.

Note: The seat should be adjusted so that the top of the torso pads are about even with the shoulders.

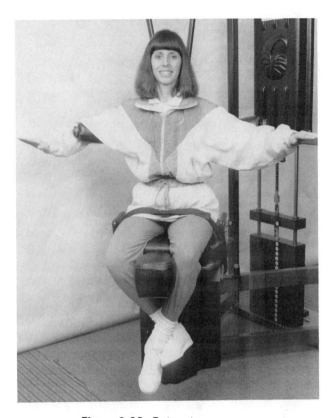

Figure 9-32. Rotary torso.

Rotary Torso Machine

The rotary torso (see Figure 9-32) is a rotary exercise that addresses the oblique muscles of the sides.

Technical Points:

1. Sit on seat with back straight and in line with machine axis of rotation.
2. Place right arm behind roller pad and left arm in front of roller pad.
3. With head, shoulders, and torso in a fixed position, turn slowly toward the left, about 45 degrees past the neutral position.
4. After a momentary pause, slowly return to starting position.
5. Repeat this movement pattern until fatigued and slowly return plates to weight stack.
6. Change seat position and repeat the above procedures moving toward the right.

Note: It is important to maintain a vertical back position throughout this exercise.

Figure 9-33. 10-degree chest.

10-Degree Chest Machine

The 10-degree chest (see Figure 9-33) is a rotary exercise that emphasizes the chest and front shoulder muscles.

Technical Points:

1. Lie on seat with feet on floor, footrest, or stool.
2. Place upper arms under roller pads.
3. Slowly raise roller pads until they meet directly above chest and hold momentarily.
4. Slowly lower roller pads until plates almost touch weight stack and repeat.

Note: The head, shoulders, and hips should remain on the seat throughout the exercise.

Figure 9-34. 40-degree chest.

40-Degree Chest Machine

The 40-degree chest (see Figure 9-34) is a rotary exercise that emphasizes the upper chest and front shoulder muscles.

Technical Points:

1. Sit on seat with feet crossed.
2. Reposition seat or use additional pad as necessary.
3. Fasten seat belt.
4. Place upper arms under roller pads.
5. Slowly raise roller pads until they meet directly above face and hold momentarily.
6. Slowly lower roller pads until plates almost touch weight stack and repeat.

Note: The head and shoulders should remain on the seat throughout the exercise.

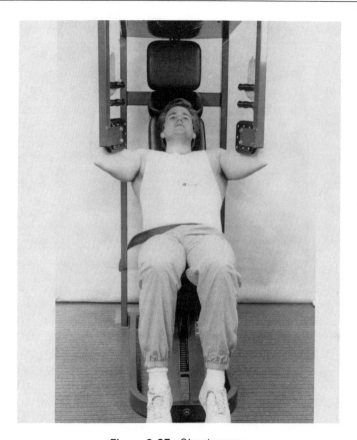

Figure 9-35. Chest cross.

Chest Cross Machine

The chest cross (see Figure 9-35) is a rotary exercise that targets the lower chest and front shoulder muscles.

Technical Points:

1. Sit on seat and align shoulder joints with machine axes of rotation.
2. Reposition seat or use additional pad as necesssary.
3. Fasten seat belt.
4. Place forearms against arm pads, with hands resting lightly on handles and upper arms parallel to floor.
5. Slowly bring arm pads together in front of face and hold momentarily.
6. Slowly move arm pads apart until plates almost touch weight stack and repeat.

Note: The head and shoulders should remain on the seat throughout the exercise.

Figure 9-36. Pullover.

Pullover Machine

The pullover (see Figure 9-36) is a rotary exercise that emphasizes the upper back and rear shoulder muscles.

Technical Points:

1. Sit on seat and align shoulder joints with machine axes of rotation.
2. Reposition seat or use additional pad as necessary.
3. Fasten seat belt.
4. Press foot lever to bring arm pads into position.
5. Place upper arms against arm pads and grip movement bar lightly with hands.
6. Slowly bring movement bar downward until it contacts seat belt and pause momentarily.
7. Slowly bring movement bar upward until muscles are comfortably stretched and repeat.
8. After final repetition, press foot lever to disengage arms and lower plates to weight stack.

Note: The downward movement should be accompanied by a slight trunk flexion to maintain support behind the lower back. The major movement force should come from the upper arms rather than from the hands.

Figure 9-37. Rowing torso.

Rowing Torso Machine

The rowing torso (see Figure 9-37) is a rotary exercise that addresses the upper back and rear shoulder muscles.

Technical Points:

1. Sit on seat with shoulder joints aligned with machine axes of rotation.
2. Use enough body pads to make a snug fit.
3. Place upper arms inside roller pads and parallel to floor.
4. Slowly move roller pads backward as far as possible and hold momentarily.
5. Slowly move roller pads forward until plates almost touch weight stack and repeat.

Note: Back should remain straight and elbows should remain high throughout this exercise.

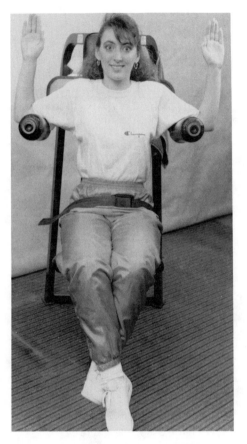

Figure 9-38. Behind neck.

Behind Neck Machine

The behind neck (see Figure 9-38) is a rotary exercise that involves the upper back muscles.

Technical Points:

1. Sit on seat and align shoulder joints with machine axes of rotation.
2. Reposition seat or use additional pad as necessary.
3. Secure seat belt.
4. Place upper arms on top of roller pads.
5. Slowly move arms downward until roller pads contact sides and pause momentarily.
6. Slowly move roller pads upward to starting position and repeat.

Note: It is important to keep the back against the seat back throughout the exercise.

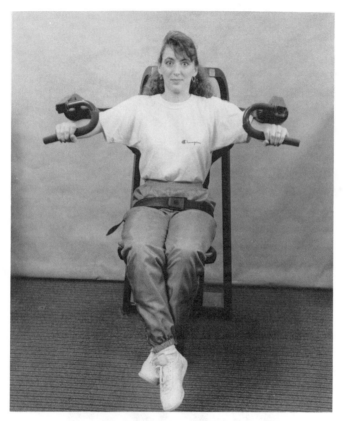

Figure 9-39. Lateral raise.

Lateral Raise Machine

The lateral raise (see Figure 9-39) is a rotary exercise that largely isolates the shoulder muscles.

Technical Points:

1. Sit on seat and align shoulder joints with machine axes of rotation.
2. Reposition seat or use additional pad as necessary.
3. Fasten seat belt.
4. Place upper arms against arm pads and grip handles loosely.
5. Slowly lift arm pads to shoulder level and hold momentarily.
6. Slowly lower arm pads until arms almost touch sides and repeat.

Note: Keep the back straight and the head in a neutral position throughout the exercise. By not letting the arms rest on the sides, constant tension is maintained on the shoulder muscles.

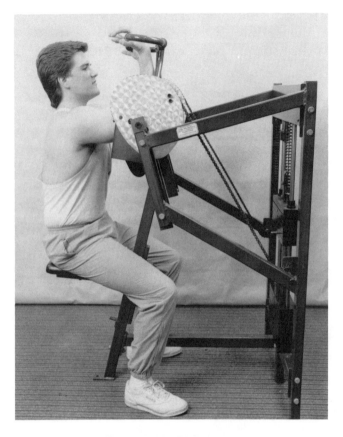

Figure 9-40. Biceps curl.

Biceps Curl Machine

The biceps curl (see Figure 9-40) is a rotary exercise that largely isolates the biceps muscles.

Technical Points:

1. Sit on seat and place elbows on pad in line with machine axes of rotation.
2. Reposition seat or use additional pad as necessary.
3. Hold handles with loose, underhand grip.
4. Slowly lift handles until elbows are fully flexed and hold momentarily.
5. Slowly lower handles until elbows are nearly extended and repeat.

Note: The shoulders should be positioned level with the elbows. For safety, it is advisable to grasp the handles with slightly bent arms before sitting down.

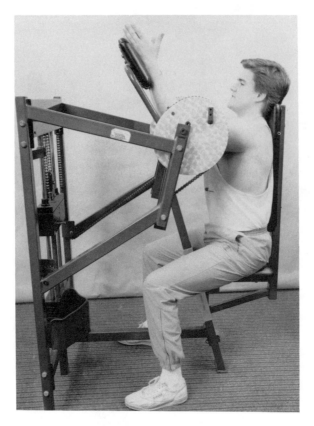

Figure 9-41. Triceps extension.

Triceps Extension Machine

The triceps extension (see Figure 9-41) is a rotary exercise that largely iso-lates the triceps muscles.

Technical Points:

1. Sit on seat and place the elbows on pad in line with machine axes of rotation.
2. Reposition seat or use additional pad as necessary.
3. Place side of hands on hand pads.
4. Slowly press hand pads forward until elbows are fully extended and hold momentarily.
5. Slowly return hand pads until elbows are comfortably flexed and repeat.

Note: The shoulders should be positioned level with the elbows. It is impor-tant to keep the elbows on the pad at all times during the exercise.

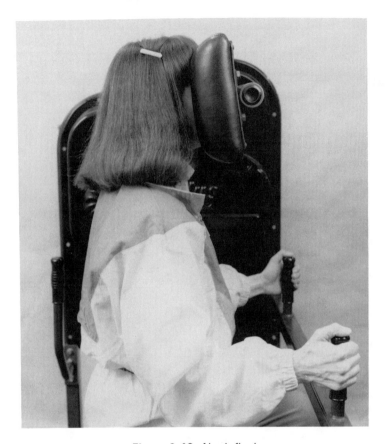

Figure 9-42. Neck flexion.

Neck Flexion Machine

The neck flexion (see Figure 9-42) is a rotary exercise that addresses the front neck muscles.

Technical Points:

1. Sit on seat and place face in center of head pads.
2. Reposition seat or use additional pad as necessary.
3. Place hands on handgrips.
4. Slowly move head forward until neck is fully flexed and pause momentarily.
5. Slowly move head backward until neck is comfortably extended and repeat.

Note: It is important to maintain the torso in an erect and stable position throughout the exercise.

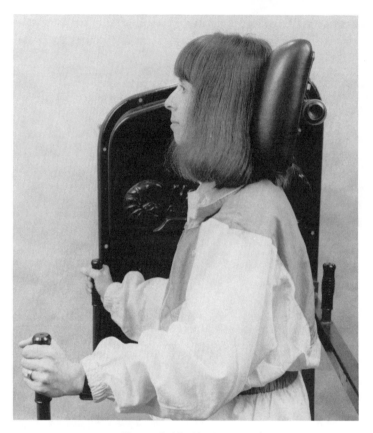

Figure 9-43. Neck extension.

Neck Extension Machine

The neck extension (see Figure 9-43) is a rotary exercise that isolates the rear neck muscles.

Technical Points:

1. Sit on seat and place head in center of pads.
2. Reposition seat or use additional pad as necessary.
3. Place hands on handgrips.
4. Slowly move head backward until neck is comfortably extended and hold momentarily.
5. Slowly move head forward until neck is comfortably flexed and repeat.

Note: It is important to maintain the torso in an erect and stable position throughout the exercise.

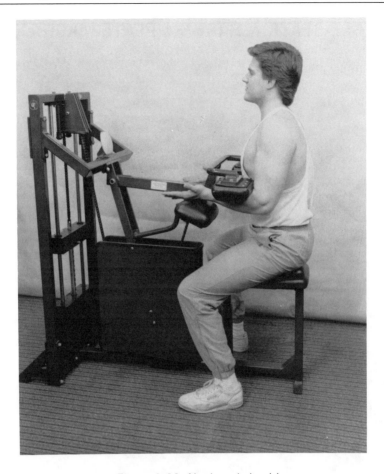

Figure 9-44. Neck and shoulder.

Neck and Shoulder Machine

The neck and shoulder (see Figure 9-44) is a rotary exercise that targets the upper trapezius muscles.

Technical Points:

1. Sit on seat and place forearms between the lifting pads with palms up.
2. Keeping the elbows in a fixed position, slowly elevate the shoulders toward the head and pause momentarily.
3. Slowly lower the shoulders to starting position and repeat.

Note: It is important to maintain the torso in an erect position throughout the exercise.

SINGLE-STATION BARBELL PLATE MACHINES

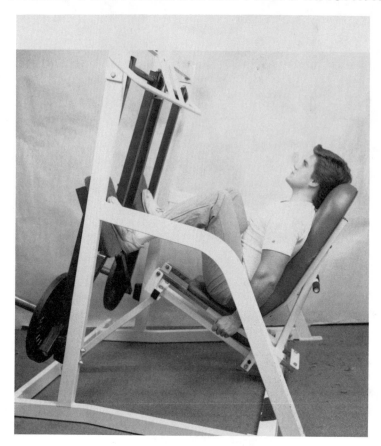

Figure 9-45. Leg press.

Leg Press

The leg press (see Figure 9-45) is a linear exercise that involves the quadriceps, hamstrings, and gluteal muscles.

Technical Points:

1. Sit securely in seat and place each foot on a foot pad.
2. Slowly push both foot pads forward to near lockout position by extending the legs.
3. Slowly return to starting position and repeat.
4. If desired, each leg may be exercised in an alternating manner.

Note: The hips and lower back should remain firmly pressed against the seat throughout the exercise.

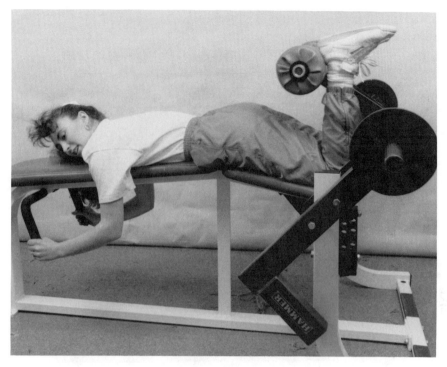

Figure 9-46. Leg curl.

Leg Curl

The leg curl (see Figure 9-46) is a rotary exercise that essentially isolates the hamstring muscles.

Technical Points:

1. Lie on seat and align knee joints with machine axes of rotation.
2. Place hands on handgrips.
3. Place ankles in neutral position behind roller pads.
4. Slowly lift roller pads until the hamstrings are fully contracted and hold momentarily
5. Slowly lower roller pads to starting position and repeat.
6. If desired, each leg may be exercised in an alternating manner.

Note: For complete contraction of the hamstring muscles, the hips must raise slightly off the support pad but should be supported as much as possible.

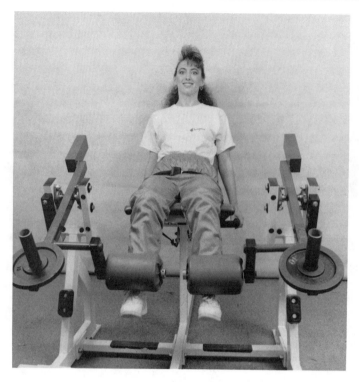

Figure 9-47. Leg extension.

Leg Extension

The leg extension (see Figure 9-47) is a rotary exercise that largely isolates the quadriceps muscles.

Technical Points:

1. Sit on seat with knee joints aligned with machine axes of rotation.
2. Adjust seat back and secure seat belt.
3. Place hands on handgrips.
4. Place ankles in neutral position behind roller pads.
5. Slowly lift roller pads until the quadriceps are fully contracted and hold momentarily.
6. Slowly lower roller pads to starting position and repeat.
7. If desired, each leg may be exercised in an alternating manner.

Note: The lower back should remain in contact with the seat back throughout the exercise.

Figure 9-48. Seated row.

Seated Row

The seated row (see Figure 9-48) is a linear exercise that involves the upper back, rear shoulder, and biceps muscles.

Technical Points:

1. Adjust seat so that shoulders are slightly higher than handgrips.
2. Grasp handgrips and place chest firmly against front pad.
3. Slowly pull handgrips to chest and pause momentarily.
4. Slowly return handgrips to starting position.
5. If desired, each side may be exercised in an alternating manner.

Note: The chest should remain in contact with the front pad throughout this exercise.

Figure 9-49. Decline press.

Decline Press

The decline press (see Figure 9-49) is a linear exercise that involves the lower chest, front shoulder, and triceps muscles.

Technical Points:

1. Adjust seat so that handgrips are at midchest level.
2. Secure seat belt and grasp handgrips.
3. Slowly push handgrips forward until arms are nearly fully extended.
4. Slowly return to starting position and repeat.
5. If desired, each side may be exercised in an alternating manner.

Note: The back should remain in contact with the seat back throughout the exercise.

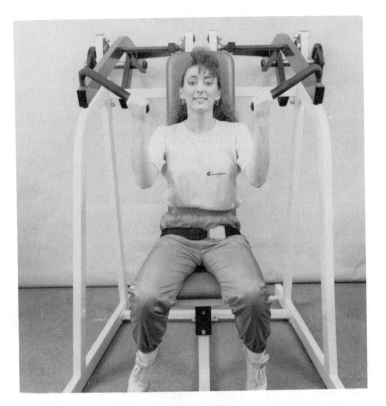

Figure 9-50. Pulldown.

Pulldown

The pulldown (see Figure 9-50) is a linear exercise that targets the upper back, rear shoulder, and biceps muscles.

Technical Points:

1. Adjust seat so that arms are fully extended in the up position.
2. Secure seat belt and grasp handles with palms facing inward.
3. Slowly pull handles to shoulders and pause momentarily.
4. Slowly return handles to starting position and repeat.
5. If desired, each side may be exercised in an alternating manner.

Note: The back should remain relatively straight throughout this exercise.

Figure 9-51. Incline press.

Incline Press

The incline press (see Figure 9-51) is a linear exercise that involves the upper chest, front shoulder, and triceps muscles.

Technical Points:

1. Adjust seat so that handgrips are at shoulder level.
2. Slowly push handgrips upward until arms are nearly fully extended.
3. Slowly return to starting position and repeat.
4. If desired, each side may be exercised in an alternating manner.

Note: The back should remain in contact with the seat back throughout the exercise.

Figure 9-52. Triceps pressdown.

Triceps Pressdown

The triceps pressdown (see Figure 9-52) is a rotary exercise that essentially isolates the triceps muscles.

Technical Points:

1. Stand inside machine frame and grasp handles with an overhand grip.
2. Bring elbows to sides.
3. Slowly push handles downward until arms are nearly extended.
4. Slowly return handles to starting position.
5. If desired, each arm may be exercised in an alternating manner.

Note: The back should remain erect and the elbows should be close to the sides throughout the exercise.

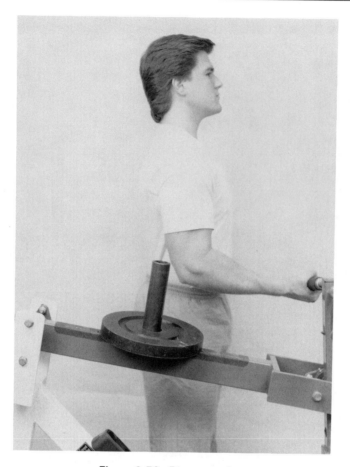

Figure 9-53. Biceps curl.

Biceps Curl

The biceps curl (see Figure 9-53) is a rotary exercise that targets the biceps muscles.

Technical Points:

1. Stand beside machine and grasp handle with right hand.
2. Slowly lift handle until elbow is fully flexed and hold momentarily.
3. Slowly lower handle until elbow is nearly extended and repeat.
4. After completing set, perform the same procedures with the left arm.

Note: The back should remain erect and the elbow should be firmly pressed against the side throughout the exercise.

MULTI-STATION WEIGHT-STACK MACHINES

Figure 9-54. Leg press.

Leg Press Station

The leg press (see Figure 9-54) is a linear exercise that involves the quadriceps, hamstrings, and gluteal muscles.

Technical Points:

1. Sit securely in seat with feet evenly placed on foot pads.
2. Slowly push foot pads forward to near lockout position by extending the legs.
3. Slowly return to starting position and repeat.

Note: The hips and lower back should remain firmly pressed against the seat throughout the exercise.

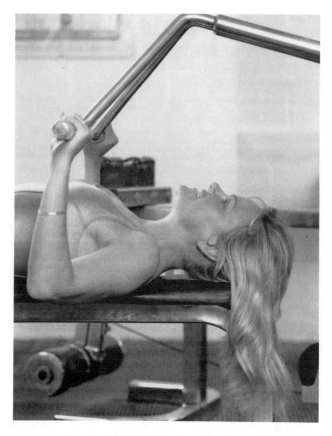

Figure 9-55. Bench press.

Bench Press Station

The bench press (see Figure 9-55) is a linear exercise that works the chest, front shoulder, and triceps muscles.

Technical Points:

1. Lie on bench with feet on floor and hands comfortably spaced on handles.
2. Slowly push handles upward to near lockout position.
3. Slowly lower handles to starting position and repeat.

Note: The head, shoulders, and hips should remain on the bench through-out the exercise.

Figure 9-56. Low row.

Low Row Station

The low row (see Figure 9-56) is a linear exercise that works the upper back, rear shoulder, and biceps muscles.

Technical Points:

1. Sit on floor and hold bar with a parallel grip.
2. Slowly pull bar to chest and pause momentarily.
3. Slowly return bar to starting position and repeat.

Note: The back should remain vertical and stable throughout the exercise.

Figure 9-57. Standing press.

Standing Press Station

The standing press (see Figure 9-57) is a linear exercise that involves the shoulder, trapezius, and triceps muscles.

Technical Points:

1. Assume staggered stance with hands comfortably spaced on handles.
2. Slowly push handles upward to near lockout position.
3. Slowly lower handles to starting position and repeat.

Note: The back should remain as straight as possible throughout the exercise.

Figure 9-58. Lat pulldown.

Lat Pulldown Station

The lat pulldown (see Figure 9-58) is a linear exercise that works the upper back, rear shoulder, and biceps muscles.

Technical Points:

1. Kneel on floor and hold bar with an underhand grip.
2. Slowly pull bar to chest and pause momentarily.
3. Slowly return bar to starting position and repeat.

Note: The back should remain as straight as possible throughout the exercise.

Figure 9-59. Biceps curl.

Biceps Curl Station

The biceps curl (see Figure 9-59) is a rotary exercise that emphasizes the biceps muscles.

Technical Points:

1. Assume shoulder-width stance and hold bar with an underhand grip.
2. Slowly curl bar to chest level and pause momentarily.
3. Slowly lower bar to starting position and repeat.

Note: It is important to keep the torso erect and the elbows stabilized against the sides throughout the exercise.

Figure 9-60. Triceps pressdown.

Triceps Pressdown Station

The triceps pressdown (see Figure 9-60) is a rotary exercise that emphasizes the triceps muscles.

Technical Points:

1. Assume shoulder-width stance and hold bar with a close, overhand grip.
2. Bring bar to starting position below chin.
3. Slowly press bar downward until elbows are fully extended.
4. Slowly return bar to starting position and repeat.

Note: It is important to keep the torso erect and the elbows stabilized against the sides throughout the exercise.

Appendix

Strength Training Logbook

Date _____ Start Time _____
Finish Time _____ Workout Time _____

Exercise:	_____	Exercise:	_____	Exercise:	_____
Weight load:	_____	Weight load:	_____	Weight load:	_____
Repetitions:	_____	Repetitions:	_____	Repetitions:	_____
Notes:	_____	Notes:	_____	Notes:	_____

Exercise:	_____	Exercise:	_____	Exercise:	_____
Weight load:	_____	Weight load:	_____	Weight load:	_____
Repetitions:	_____	Repetitions:	_____	Repetitions:	_____
Notes:	_____	Notes:	_____	Notes:	_____

Exercise:	_____	Exercise:	_____	Exercise:	_____
Weight load:	_____	Weight load:	_____	Weight load:	_____
Repetitions:	_____	Repetitions:	_____	Repetitions:	_____
Notes:	_____	Notes:	_____	Notes:	_____

Exercise:	_____	Exercise:	_____	Exercise:	_____
Weight load:	_____	Weight load:	_____	Weight load:	_____
Repetitions:	_____	Repetitions:	_____	Repetitions:	_____
Notes:	_____	Notes:	_____	Notes:	_____

Rest period since last workout: _____
Body weight: _____
Measurements: _____

Feelings: Strong   Average   Weak
              Energetic   Average   Tired
              Enthusiastic   Average   Unenthusiastic